The Era after the Baroque

Music and the Fine Arts 1750-1900

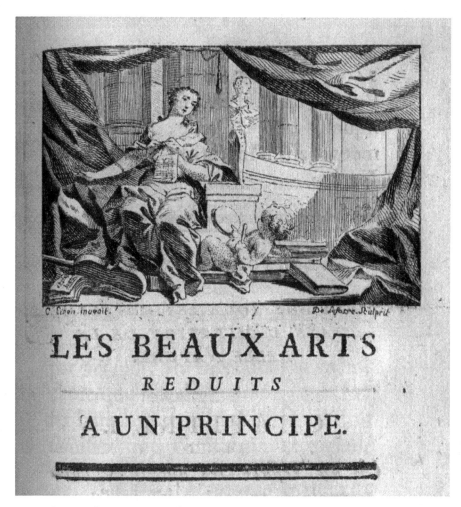

LES BEAUX ARTS
REDUITS
A UN PRINCIPE.

Vignette from Batteux's *Les Beaux Arts reduits à un meme principe* (1747)

Batteux placed his work under the aegis of Calliope, daughter of Zeus and Mnemosyne (Memory). Calliope, whose name means *beautiful voice* or *beautiful song* was the muse of epic poetry. She was the mother of Orpheus who could enchant men and animals by his singing and by his playing of the lyre. This vignette is described by Batteux, as "Calliope sings verses of poetry; a small genie marks the rhythm." The instrument held by her companion is the kithara appropriate to the singing of epic verse.

The Era after the Baroque

Music and the Fine Arts 1750-1900

by

Robert Tallant Laudon

MONOGRAPHS IN MUSICOLOGY No. 13

PENDRAGON PRESS

HILLSDALE, NEW YORK

Other Titles in the Series MONOGRAPHS IN MUSICOLOGY

No. 2   La Statira *by Pietro Ottoboni and Alessandro Scarlatti The Textual Sources* by William C. Holmes (1983)

No. 6   *The Art of Noises* by Luigi Russolo (1987)

No. 9   *Piano and Song (Didactic and Polemical)* by Friedrich Wieck *The Collected Writings of Clara Schumann's Father and Only Teacher* (1988)

No. 10   *Confraternity and Carnevale at San Giovanni Evangelista, Florence, 1820-1924* by Aubrey S. Garlington (1992)

No. 11   *Franz Schubert's Music in Performance Compositional Ideals, Notational Intent, Historical Realities, Pedagogical Foundations* by David Montgomery (2003)

No. 12   *Revolving Embrace The Waltz as Sex, Steps, and Sound* by Sevin H. Yaramin (2002)

Library of Congress Cataloging in Publication Data

Laudon, Robert T.

The era after the Baroque : music and the fine arts 1750-1900 / by Robert Tallant Laudon.

p. cm. -- (Monographs in musicology ; no. 13)

Includes bibliographical references and index.

ISBN 978-1-57647-124-1

1. Music--19th century--History and criticism. 2. Music--18th century--History and criticism. 3. Art and music. I. Title.

ML193.L38 2008

780.9'033--dc22

2008013536

Contents

Illustrations

Musical Examples

Preface

What shall we call the era in western music history from 1750 to 1900? Listeners and scholars alike treasure the works of its great composers: Mozart, Beethoven, Chopin, Wagner, Tchaikovsky. A powerfully symbolic name, though—analogous to "baroque" for the previous era—still eludes us.

We refer constantly to two trends, classical and romantic, which have substantive meaning for various composers' orientations and for ways of performing the music. But these two terms—whether understood as indicating consecutive or overlapping trends—do not plainly suggest the two main events of the age: the industrial revolution, and the democratic political upheavals of 1776, 1789, and 1848. Also, they do not acknowledge an emerging sense of humanity or the excitement of a passionate audience seeking recognition and expression.

This extended essay proposes a powerful symbol for the new era while at the same time keeping traditional terminology intact. It looks at the age in a primarily positive manner while still acknowledging its darker aspects. In particular, it evokes the sphere of the newly recognized system of "fine arts" and therefore has resonances for the visual and literary arts in addition to its primary focus on music.

It advances an expressive ideal that is traced in both vocal and instrumental music during that century and a half. It stresses that music was not an art unique and set apart but rather participated in the great dissemination of education and artistic opportunity that was then emerging in the context of an increasingly human-centered concept of freedom.

Acknowledgments

Thanks are extended to musicologists Ralph Locke, David Grayson, Leon Plantinga, DonnaMae Gustafson, and Stanislav Tuksar; to composer Dominick Argento; to pianist Louise Guhl; to writer Georgia Greeley; and to several anonymous readers. All have been exceedingly helpful but are not, of course, responsible for any insufficiencies that still remain. Special gratitude goes to the librarians of the University of Minnesota, the New York Public Library, Washington University at St. Louis, the Pierpont Morgan Library, the Bibliothèque de l' Opéra (Paris), and the Newberry Library. Several librarians have helped beyond the call of duty: Susan Rippley and Timothy Maloney of the University of Minnesota, John Bidwell of The Morgan Library, Jill Gage of the Newberry Library, and Erin Davis of Washington University,

1. Naming the Era

Historians have divided their raw material for western Europe and those areas dependent upon western European traditions into extended eras, each representing a norm of society, style, and thought. They have then subdivided these large eras into shorter time spans, generally called periods. Our terminology for eras derives from a number of sources, most frequently from nineteenth-century historical research. Several terms such as Medieval, Renaissance, and Baroque are in current use. Two even achieved their status after first being used in a pejorative fashion.

"Medieval," has the fundamental meaning of "Middle Ages." This word, by itself, denotes a time span but very few stylistic messages; those have accrued by usage. "Renaissance," has a basic meaning of "rebirth" and carried an ideal with it, a time of rebirth of the human spirit evident previously in classical Greece and Rome. From its initial concept, in the fifteenth and sixteenth centuries as a literary emergence of humanism, it has come to denote both a time span and a stylistic ideal. "Baroque," on the other hand, derives in modern usage from style analysis, particularly as Baroque contrasts with Renaissance style in the visual arts. It was first formulated in the work of the art historian Heinrich Wölfflin[1] but its meaning has broadened as public, scholars, and performers have discovered its special wonders and depth of thought.

Manfred Bukofzer used the scheme of era, period, and comprehensive name effectively in his path-breaking study of music in the Baroque Era.[2] He recognized both the advantages and disadvantages of generic terms such as baroque. These terms cannot have absolutely precise definitions. He knew that "the concrete life of a period knows internal contradictions, conflicts of prevalent and suppressed ideas, survivals from the preceding and anticipations of the following periods," however "in spite of these complexities, the prevalent ideas of an era stand out and must receive the main attention."[3] So indeed, baroque—originally referring to an irregular pearl or to a tortured syllogism—has now become a widely accepted symbol of an era.

---

[1]Heinrich Wölfflin, *Renaissance und Barock* (Munich: T. Ackermann, 1888); *Kunstgeschichtliche Grundbegriffe* (Munich: F. Bruckman, 1915).
[2]Manfred Bukofzer, *Music in the Baroque Era: From Monteverdi to Bach* (New York: Norton, 1947). He divided the entire era into three smaller periods, Early, Middle, and Late Baroque.
[3]Bukofzer, *Baroque Era*, 2-3.

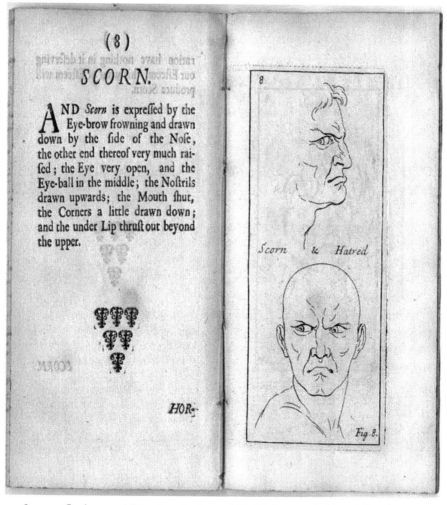

Scorn, *Conference of Monsieur Le Brun, Chief Painter to the French King...upon EXPRESSION, General and Particular, translated from the French, and Adorned with 43 Copper-Plates) (1701).*
Courtesy Special Collections and Rare Books
Libraries of the University of Minnesota at Minneapolis

Bukofzer embraced both the view of a *generalist*, aware of the over-arching concept, and that of the *specialist*, concerned with a wealth of detail and a close examination of each small unit of the unfolding fabric of history. Obviously the present essay adopts the generalist view, and as such, has all the advantages and pitfalls of that approach. It provides a broad concept that does not attack prevailing thought but instead seeks to expand our conceptual horizons.

Claude Palisca, in a later study, showed a way to resolve some problems inherent in identifying a musical era solely by details of musical construction. He maintained, justly in my view, that baroque style should be considered "unified and delimited more by an expressive ideal than by a consistent body of musical techniques."[4] He did not deny the importance of techniques such as chord structure, harmonic progression, basso continuo, and figural patterns but placed these within his larger concept of the arousal of the affections or passions, a topic that had been advanced by Descartes[5] in a highly influential treatise of 1650. An affection was caused by the balance or imbalance of animal spirits in the body and especially as they react on the brain. The affections were thought to be quite stable, exerting their influence until some outside force changed the passion. In art works generally and in music particularly, this meant that one passion at a time was presented, the so-called doctrine of the single affection.[6]

Such a belief in the affections led Charles Le Brun, chief painter to Louis XIV, to initiate in 1667 a series of conferences, one of which is preserved in posthumous publications from 1698 and into the 1700s, a group of sketches and descriptions showing the facial look (illustration opposite page) of each of the affections, a presentation almost like a recipe book, a dictionary of the passions[7] which gives the present-day connoisseur of that age a remarkable compendium of the affections and their representation in their simplest, most direct, form. Le Brun did not consider in this particular treatise the uses of color, design, form, costume, light, shadow, brush strokes, and more items that had their role in representing the passions.

[4]Claude Palisca, *Baroque Music* (Englewood Cliffs, N. J.: Prentice Hall, 1991), 6.

[5]The most influential treatise on the passions or affections (both terms were used) was by René Descartes, *Les Passions de l'âme* (Amsterdam: Louys Elzevier, 1650) and various following editions including one in Latin. Descartes believed that there were only a few primitive passions: wonder, love, hatred, desire, joy, and madness. Other passions came from mixtures of these.

[6]This need not be the simplest possible affection. By use of rhetorical devices such as hypotyposis, vivid description, or by movements of climax or anticlimax, anabasis or catabasis, and others, Bach created complex "pictures" and with them a complex affection of urgent devotion. The duet in Cantata 78, "Wir eilen mit schwachen, doch emsigen Schritten," for instance, depicts the *footsteps* in the bass parts, and the *hastening* by faster moving ascending duet voices, and even the *feeble* but *diligent* quality by only the slightest movement around a single note.

[7]The system of facial expressions showing the passions may seem bizarre to modern thinkers but work in evolution and in psychology has given support to the proposition that Le Brun advanced. Darwin tried to compare emotions in man and other animals and found similarities. The psychologist, Paul Ekman, has devoted the major portion of his career to the study of emotion and its facial characteristics, see *Emotion in the Human Face: Guide-lines for Research* (New York: Pergamon, 1972); *What the Face Reveals*, 2nd ed. (New York: Oxford, 2005); *Emotions Inside Out: 130 Years after Darwin's The Expression of the Emotions in Man and Animals* (New York: New York Academy of Sciences, 2003); and articles such as "Facial Expressions of Emotions: New Findings, New Questions," *Psychological Science* 3 (1992), 34-38. He has shown that facial expressions for anger, happiness, sadness, disgust, fear and surprise, are recognized in many differing cultures around the world and seem inherent in the human psyche probably as a result of our evolutionary past.

Musicians in their art had a similar wealth of stylistic possibilities that could give music a meaning beyond technical perfection. Two German treatises dealt with the issue.[8] The author of the most complete compilation of the affects in music, Johann Mattheson, in *Der vollkommene Capellmeister* (1739), began by considering the "the effects of well-disposed sounds on the emotions and the soul."[9] He referred directly to Descartes and drew musical parallels.

> Since, for example, joy is an *expansion* of our vital spirits *(Lebens Geister)*, it follows sensibly and naturally that this affect is best expressed in large and expanded intervals. Sadness, on the other hand, is a *contraction* of those same subtle parts of our bodies. It is, therefore, easy to see that the narrowest intervals are the most suitable."[10]

Later in a longer section, he described the various genres, particularly dances, and ascribed to each its particular affect before discussing its construction. The minuet, for example, "has no other affect than *moderate gaiety*," the gavotte's "affect is truly *jubilant joy (jauchzende Freude)*," and the rigaudon's affection is "one of *flirtatious pleasantry (tändelden Schertz)*."[11]

Baroque artists, writers, and orators used yet another device in their pursuit of an expressive ideal: *ornament*, expressed in florid handwriting, architectural flourishes, high flown speech brimming with rhetorical devices, and elaborate settings in the theater. The art of music similarly employed ornaments—noted by special signs or by expected improvisation. They were intended to "grace" the line.[12] Simplicity did exist from time to time but, for the most part, ornamentation was integral to the style.[13]

---

[8]Johann David Heinichen, *Der General Bass in der Komposition* (Dresden, 1728); reprint edition by Georg Olms Verlag (1969). In the introduction to this work, Heinichen presented the musical representation of the affects within operatic arias. See George J. Buelow's "The Loci Topici and Affect in late baroque Music: Heinichen's practical Demonstration," *The Music Review* 27 (1966), 161-76; Johann Mattheson, *Der vollkommene Capellmeister* (1839); reprint ed. by Margarete Reimann (Kassel: Bärenreiter, 1954). A revised translation with critical commentary by Ernest C. Harriss has been published by UMI Research Press, Ann Arbor, Mich., c. 1981. See Hans Lenneberg's "Johann Mattheson on Affect and Rhetoric in Music," *Journal of Music Theory* 2 (1958).

[9]*Der vollkommene Capellmeister*, Part I, Chapter III; translation is by Hans Lenneberg, "Mattheson," 51.

[10]*Capellmeister*, I, III; Lenneberg, "Mattheson," 51-52.

[11]*Capellmeister*, II, XIII; Lenneberg, "Mattheson," 57, 59, 60.

[12]The English term for a musical ornament was "grace." The French was "*agrément*," a noun derived from the verb *agréer* meaning to "receive favorably" and "to like;" the nominative form indicates "approval and pleasure." Formal speech in this day used rhetorical devices, conceits, and involved expressions. It would seem that if an idea were important, it was necessary to express it in a lofty way. In a similar way, graces were integral to musical ideas.

[13]These devices of musical speech are covered in Mattheson's *Capellmeister* and in Heinichen's *Der General Bass*. Both of these authors pay close attention as to how the complete composition is fashioned in addition to the original invention of a theme.

The doctrine of the affections and the consistent use of ornament suited well an era in which the first two estates, the nobility and the clergy, were controlling figures in life of the times. Enormous changes, however, became evident around 1750 when those estates saw their hegemony begin to slip. In the latter half of the eighteenth century, two revolutions, the democratic and the industrial, confirmed that a new era was upon western Europe. The name, or at least a one-word name, for this age is still in doubt.

Bukofzer, noted as a historian of the Baroque Era, later taught a class covering the shorter Classic Period and produced a valuable syllabus for that time frame but did not move on to consider what might be the best way in which to conceive of the large era, the years 1750 to 1900, following the Baroque Age. In fact, despite the current interest in historiography, no one-word term is currently in use for music or the other arts.

Several decades ago, Friedrich Blume recognized the inclusive and intertwined nature of classic and romantic styles.

> "Classicism" and "Romanticism" are just two aspects of one and the same musical phenomenon and of one and the same historical period. In terms of chronology, the two labels signify one self-contained age of the history of music, in terms of style, they mark the two facets of this age, the two trends operating within the one fundamental idea of form and expression. There is neither a "Classic" nor a "Romantic" style in music. Both aspects and both trends are continually merging into one. And as there are no discernible styles, there can neither be a clearly definable borderline between Classicism and Romanticism nor a distinct chronology of when the one or the other begins or ends.[14]

Blume, however, made no attempt to move beyond the dual terminology. Yet changes are being offered.[15] A recent step to expand traditional boundaries lies in the concept of the "long century,"[16] an extension of the actual chronological limits of the nineteenth century to accommodate a broader view for articles intended for journals devoted to that century.

[14]The question was broached in Friedrich Blume's articles in *Die Musik in Geschichte und Gegenwart* in 1958 and 1963, reworked and translated by M. D. Herter Norton, *Classic and Romantic Music, A Comprehensive Survey* (New York: Norton, 1970). The quotation comes from the two-page preface of this latter work.

[15]Among recent works discussing "classic" are Abigail Chantler, "The Classical Period: A Musicological Misnomer," *Ad Parnassum A Journal of Eighteenth- and Nineteenth-Century Instrumental Music*, vol. 2/1 (Oct. 2003), 121-42, and Leon Plantinga, Review of Anselm Gerhard, *London und der Klassizismus in der Musik*, same journal, 158-65.

[16]See, among others, the re-established *Music Review*, now the *Nineteenth-Century Music Review*, which will recognize the span 1789-1914 and *19th Century Music* 25, nos. 2-3 (fall 2001-spring 2002), which is devoted to the "long century" of 1780-1920. David Blackbourn has even titled his history of Germany, 1780-1918, *The Long Century*. The Scribner publication *Europe 1450 to 1789: Encyclopedia of the Early Modern World* is to be followed by a similar publication for the period 1789 to 1914.

Blume also made no attempt to incorporate another pertinent stylistic term, *galant*, into his view since, at the time of his writing, a complete study of that period was lacking. Only recently Daniel Heartz has supplied that information in an organized and magisterial fashion.[17] *Galant* as a stylistic term is essential to understanding those sixty years in which the baroque style was fading and the new style was in the ascendant.[18]

While classic and romantic, the current terms, do accurately present the change from a balanced to a more unbridled type of expression, they convey very little of the intrinsic character of the society established after the Baroque Era. They instead convey the dynamics that could characterize almost any age: a thesis/antithesis. It would be almost like referring to the Baroque Age as the Antico-Moderno Age or the Prima-Seconda Practtiche Era. A synthesis is missing.

At times we have been so inundated with the negative features of the nineteenth-century that we may question whether a synthesis is even possible. We now realize, however, that advances of technology, science, and medicine in the new era made life less of a struggle and the plight of mankind less dependent on unknown forces. The condition of the ordinary person greatly improved from 1750 to 1900 in ways that would have been nearly impossible for a seventeenth-century man to envision. Material advance and human aspects intertwined with each other even as they evolved sometimes independently. The historian/philosopher of science, Jacob Bronowski, described the situation thus:

> We take it for granted now that science has a social responsibility. That idea would not have occurred to Newton or to Galileo. They thought of science as an account of the world as it is, and the only responsibility that they acknowledged was to tell the truth. The idea that science is a social enterprise is modern, and it began with the Industrial Revolution. We are surprised that we cannot trace a social sense further back, because we nurse the illusion that the Industrial Revolution ended a golden age.[19]

Beyond the vast changes in the material world, the guiding principle of the new age is found in a sense of *humanity* recognized as part of the social

---

[17]Daniel Heartz, *Music in European Capitals: The Galant Style, 1720-1780* (New York: Norton, 2003).

[18]Heartz recognizes a first phase (to 1750) and second phase (after 1750) of galant style. He places the decline of the galant style around 1780. This coincides with a historian's view of the beginning of the most active phase of the industrial revolution. E. J. Hobsbawm, *The Age of Revolution, 1789-1848* (New York: New American Library, 1962), 45, in discussing the earlier starting point of the industrial revolution, maintains that the forces already in motion gathered momentum around 1780. I am using the date of 1750 as a starting date for the era in full recognition that, while that is an appropriate date for the changes in society and for the broad picture that I present, the era was still aborning.

[19] Jacob Bronowski, *The Ascent of Man* (Boston: Little Brown, 1973), 259.

dynamic of life. The human and humane aspects of the democratic revolution expressed in mottos—Liberty, Equality, Fraternity—Life, Liberty, and the Pursuit of Happiness—The Torch of Reason—began to supplement the teachings that had for ages been centered in the church. Still the church itself was changing. New faiths were attracting the common folk. Many devout people, believers in the "religion of the heart," were leading the way toward social action, republicanism, and a more egalitarian age. Slavery was abolished or was on the way to abolition in western Europe.

Individual devoted people began to be concerned with the most vulnerable members of society: women and children. In 1770 until his death in 1826, Johann Friedrich Oberlin, a pastor working in a poverty-stricken group of villages in the Vosges Mountains, combined his religious faith with republican ardor and thereby transformed residents lives by many initiatives. Prime among these were infant schools for children as young as three or four, followed by compulsory education to age sixteen—these standards at a time when in England children were "put into the mills" by age ten.[20] In 1794 Oberlin won an accolade from the National Convention for his championship of the French language that removed the children from the handicap of a patois. In 1818 he was awarded the medal of the Royal Agricultural Society. "A year and a half later, Oberlin, to his own surprise…received the highest distinction in the power of the nation, the Cross of the Legion of Honor."[21] About the same time as Oberlin's initiatives, Johann Heinrich Pestalozzi, who had been brought up as an orphan, established a school for deprived children and gradually formed a whole theory of teaching which in turn inspired his student, Friedrich Fröbel who started the kindergarten movement, a foundation stone of childhood education.

It had been part of social life to savor the thrill of public executions. Now people were beginning to forsake that amusement.[22] A few concerned citizens were even crusading against cruelty to animals. "Humanity Martin," [Richard Martin, Member of Parliament] led the charge in 1822 for an anti-cruelty law and, in 1824, with a group of associates, founded the Royal Society for the Prevention of Cruelty to Animals, the first such organization in the world.[23]

Within the "lower orders," self-help groups began to spread literacy and leadership. Among the pioneering foster fathers of this movement was Benjamin Franklin who as early as 1727 gathered a group of workers into a discussion group, the Junta. From Franklin's fertile and active mind came a host of

[20]John W. Kurtz, *John Frederic Oberlin* (Boulder, Colorado: Westview, 1976), 74. For a short summary of his life and endeavors see Kurtz's "What's in a Name: Why Oberlin?" *Oberlin Alumni Magazine*, 68 (November/December 1972): 4-9.

[21]Kurtz, *Oberlin*, 277-78.

[22]Peter Gay, *The Enlightenment: An Interpretation*, volume 2 (New York: Norton, 1977), 16-17.

[23]See the entry in *Brewer's Dictionary of Phrase & Fable*, ed. Ivor H. Evans (New York: Harper & Row, 1981) and the RSPCA website.

innovations: a lending library, a fire brigade, night watchmen, a hospital, a militia, a college, and the American Philosophical Society. Soon he was well recognized in Europe, particularly in England and France where he lived for extended periods. Similar clubs and libraries for self-improvement, some even formed after Franklin's example, grew up in Scotland and England.[24]

A veritable mania for self-education began to spread for those of the artisan class eager to rise in the world. In France, "towns everywhere had reading clubs, rental libraries, and bookshops where customers could read at their leisure for a modest fee without necessarily buying."[25]

> Marginal dealers often established such societies by making their stock double as the holding of a library, ordering an assortment of journals, and setting up a reading room behind their shop. The members paid a subscription fee, sometimes only 3 livres a month (a day's wages for a skilled artisan); and in return they could read all they wanted.[26]

We will notice frequently such a devotion to education in the succeeding pages of this essay.

Literary people extolled the new feeling for mankind. Mercy, pity, peace and love envisioned by Blake became a *divine image.*

> For Mercy has a human heart,
>
> Pity a human face,
>
> And Love, the human form divine,
>
> And Peace, the human dress.[27]

He concluded that where these human virtues dwell "there God is dwelling too."

Only by recognizing this ideal and by using it as a measuring stick could Blake judge what were the horrors of reality. He knew both innocence and experience. Much of the shock that people of the span from 1750 to 1900 felt as they viewed slavery, exhausting hours, poverty, and exploitation of children arose from this newly-aroused sense of humanity. People had become sensitive to injustice that they might have formerly accepted as yet another one of life's numerous burdens.

---

[24]Jonathan Rose, *The Intellectual Life of the British Working Classes* (New Haven: Yale University, 2001), Chap. 2.

[25]Leo Damrosch, *Jean-Jacques Rousseau: Restless Genius* (Boston: Houghton Mifflin, 2001), 325.

[26]Robert Darnton, *The Forbidden Best-Sellers of Pre-Revolutionary France* (New York: Norton, 1995), 45.

[27]William Blake, *Songs of Innocence* (published 1789).

There was a time prior to this era in which mankind remained somewhat immune to ills visited upon it.

Near the end of the sixteenth century, Montaigne, who was not a notably cruel man and who recommended that children be treated with kindness, recalled that he had lost "two or three children in their infancy, not without regret but without great sorrow." Montaigne's failure to mourn is less shocking than his inability to remember just how many of his children had died."[28]

Blake, instead, recognized the vulnerable ones: the little girl lost, the little boy lost, the little girl found, the little boy found.

Peter Gay in a monumental study seeking "the spirit of the age" explained the situation thus:

Men had been charitable before this time, obviously. They had given alms to the poor and felt pity for the unfortunate. What was new about eighteenth-century humanity was that it formed part of the general recovery of nerve: its optimistic decency was grounded in the rational foundations of scientific improvement as much as in religious prescription. Generosity was a luxury a progressive society could afford.[29]

Gay recognized the numerous problems standing in the way of progressive action.

As society grew more complex—one of the prices exacted by modernity—class barriers grew steeper, mines and factories voracious for the labor of children and the respectable classes resisted the aspirations of the lower orders.[30]

Yet despite reaction and opposing forces "in general, humanity was acquiring the status of a practical virtue."[31]

The great technological/scientific changes and the new concept of humanity are the two indispensable criteria that must be incorporated as we seek an inclusive single term, an umbrella concept, a synthesis that could be effectively used for this extended era of 1750 to 1900. Such a term would not supplant but include the terms classic and romantic so useful when discussing style and performance. Those terms derive from German literary and musical

---

[28]Gay, *Enlightenment*, 35.
[29]Gay, *Enlightenment*, 30. Note the recognition of both science and religion, the dual nature of the new society.
[30]Gay, *Enlightenment*, 35.
[31]Gay, *Enlightenment*, 36.

usage and—considering the important heritage of music developed within the German-speaking world—they have deserved currency.[32] They will be incorporated within the present proposal.

The time has come to give music a place within a larger historical sphere. The postulated term for the era—described in the next two chapters—is intended as a symbol to delineate a historical movement, an evolving material society with new ideals of life expressed in a music that moves away from the noble Baroque into a different sphere.

[32]Many are seeking a way out of the confusion that surrounds this classification scheme. See James Webster's "Between Enlightenment and Romanticism in Music History: 'First Viennese Modernism' and the Delayed Nineteenth Century," *19th Century Music* 25 (Fall/Spring 2001-02), 108-26 and especially Figure 1: Some Periodizations of eighteenth-century music.

2. The Proposal: The First Main Theme

The name that I propose for this historical movement is the Promethean Era, a term derived from Greek legend. It takes its name from the Titan, Prometheus, son of Iapetus and Themis.[1] The adjective "promethean" traditionally carried meanings such as "pertaining to Prometheus who stole fire from heaven"[2] or "pertaining to, or resembling Prometheus, in his skill, art, or punishment,"[3] the emphasis being on the Titan himself. Over the years definitions and connotations have strayed some distance from the original meaning. In this essay the Titan's name will be used in the traditional sense to refer to one who stole fire (and by extension technology) from the realm of the gods and brought it to earth for the benefit of mankind at a time when humans were untutored and in great need of means of improvement.

Aeschylus in *Prometheus Bound* has the Titan proclaim, in two great soliloquies,[4] both the potency of fire *and* the necessity of education, technology *and* humanity.[5] All too often Prometheus has been associated solely with technology and has acquired the connotation of "unfettered power and

[1]In the Aeschylus drama, Prometheus acknowledges Themis as his mother. Other sources sometimes state that his mother was Asia. It is from Themis, a Titan, Mother-Goddess, and Deity of the Delphic Oracle (before Apollo), that Prometheus, the forethinker, gained his power to know foreordained events.

[2]Noah Webster, *An American Dictionary of the English Language* (New Haven: Hezekiah Howe, 1828).

[3]Still used in the latest edition (1989) of the *New Oxford Dictionary*.

[4]Each soliloquy occurs at a moment of great stress for the Titan: the first after he has been chained and the second after he has refused an offer by his fellow Titan, Oceanus, to recant and reconcile with Zeus. The second soliloquy is delivered in the presence of the Oceanides, witnesses to his most private convictions.

[5]Lawrence Kramer, "The Waters of Prometheus: Nationalism and Sexuality in Wagner's *Ring*," *The Work of Opera: Genre, Nationhood, and Sexual Difference*, ed. Richard Dellamora and Daniel Fischlin (New York: Columbia University, 1997), 135-36, perceptively notes "In classical terms, Prometheus the fire-bringer is a personification of Bronze Age technology. Only much later, in the Promethean texts of European Romanticism, does the emphasis shift from material to symbolic culture, from technique to value." Kramer finds that the fire element of Prometheus "becomes expendable" within that literature as writers focus on what I am calling the "second theme." I would, however, claim that while the literary references to fire/technology begin to disappear as the new sense of humanity begins to flourish, the actuality of fire/technology is the very foundation of industrial society. It is so pervasive that it hardly needs mention except when it treads upon the ideals that are dawning.

Prometheus (Henry Fuseli, c. 1770-71)

Here a technical study becomes expressive: Fuseli and the sculptor Thomas Banks devised an artistic exercise. They placed five dots—representing the feet, hands, and head—randomly on the page and then drew a figure conforming to these restrictions. Fuseli turned the exercise into an expressive drawing of the tortured Prometheus and added the devouring eagle to the composition.[6] This procedure has some resemblance to the Chopin Etudes that are technical in conception but expressive in result.

Courtesy of the Kunstmuseum Basel, Kupferstichkabinett

[6]The "five-point game" and its place in Fuseli's development is discussed in Martin Myrone, *Henry Fuseli* (Princeton, N. J.: Princeton University Press, c. 2001), 27-29.

ambition"[7] whereas his tutoring of mankind, his blessing of the race with intelligence, his gift of letters and numbers to be their memory and even their muses' handmaid, has been neglected. Recognition of that second aspect of Prometheus lies at the heart of this essay, the very keystone of the argument. It will be treated in the following chapter.

The term, admittedly, has some accrued meanings that might confuse if not addressed explicitly here. In the twentieth century, a secondary definition "daringly original and creative" began to appear especially in concise, college, and American dictionaries. This has converted the original term to a simple adjective with only tangential reference to the Titan. "Daringly original and creative" is an aesthetic judgment, a usage that can be applied to a single work of art but which would have little or no meaning when applied to an entire era. For individuals, it could apply equally to Perotin, Machaut, Monteverdi or many others. I will avoid this preconceived judgment just as Bukofzer avoided the term High Baroque that conveys a blanket valuation and even implied that there must be some type of Low Baroque.

Yet another connotation surrounds Prometheus and promethean, the connotation of hero and heroic. The Titan can be viewed as a hero, not in the older concept of "favored by the gods," but as a hero for mankind, one who defied the gods and is to be honored for his deeds and his sacrifice. This is an important part of the concept "promethean;" however just to name him as a hero, to praise him with reiterated pomp and ceremony, brings little meaning. If we were to name the new era simply a heroic age, it would give slight significance to the multifaceted deeds, aims, and accomplishments of the composers and artists of the age from 1750 to 1900. Instead it appears that we must discover the Titan's precepts and gifts to mankind and then use these in proposing his name as a symbol for an era in history and the arts. I will draw, therefore, upon the original, more precise and detailed meanings that are best expressed in Greek drama.

Aeschylus related the myth in three plays of which only the first, *Prometheus Bound,* survives intact. The first theme is embedded in the story of how Prometheus has stolen fire from heaven. Power and Violence, agents of Zeus, ruler of the gods, drag Prometheus to the wasteland of Scythia. There, Hephaistos, god of fire and forge, much against his wishes, binds Prometheus to a rock (illustration opposite page). Bound and alone in the wilderness, Prometheus, the Forethinker—the literal meaning of his name—acknowledges his transgression and gives his reason for the theft.

---

[7]This viewpoint is unfortunate because Power is one of the agents of Zeus who binds Prometheus to the rock. Ambition is completely renounced by the Titan, his actions are selfless in the face of the suffering he knows will follow his actions. Some versions of the legend even have him creating mankind itself.

For the power, the glory I gave to human beings
I'm bound in irons.
I tracked down fire, where it springs from.
And stole it, I hid
the spark in a fennel stalk, and brought it
to human beings. Now it shines
forth: a teacher
showing all mankind the way to all the arts there are.[8]

The term "arts" which appears in the final line of this excerpt is somewhat misleading. The original Greek of Aeschylus for "teacher of the arts" was *didaskalos technes*, the first word denoting a didact, and the second word with the close English cognate of "techniques," variously translated as arts, skills, or crafts. It does not mean the modern fine arts—which were first defined in mid-eighteenth century—but means instead the useful arts.[9] It is the gift to change man's terrestrial life through technological power, the transforming force brought to earth by Prometheus whose very name became the symbol of material progress. Even the Titan's fire became a natural symbol of the new era.

The red glow has become the picture of the new age in England—in the sermons of John Wesley, and in the furnace sky of the Industrial Revolution, such as the fiery landscape of Abbeydale in Yorkshire, an early center for new processes in making iron and steel.[10]

The new age gave these practical arts, the crafts and skills that Aeschylus placed under the term *tekhne*, a favored place. The motto of Diderot, editor of the *Encyclopédie*, was indeed "être utile aux hommes," to be useful to men.[11] Skilled artisans now held an increasingly important role and were essential not only to the general populace of an evolving new society but to musicians who needed instruments that were reliable, that had greater strength of tone, and that could be manufactured in sufficient quantity to serve a growing public.

[8]Aeschylus, *Prometheus Bound*, trans. James Scully and John Herington (New York: Oxford University, 1975), 34-35 (lines 163-170). Quotations from the drama will be taken from this source unless otherwise indicated.

[9]Paul Oskar Kristeller, "The Modern System of the Arts: A Study in the History of Aesthetics," *Journal of the History of Ideas* 11 (1951): 498-505.

[10]Jacob Bronowski, *The Ascent of Man* (Boston: Little, Brown, 1973), 272.

[11]Diderot, Lettre à Voltaire, 19 février 1758, *Correspondance*, vol. 2 (Paris: Édition de Minuit, 1956), 39. See also his entry on "Art" in the *Encyclopédie* where he discusses the values given to the useful arts as opposed to the liberal arts. This matter is discussed in Arthur M. Wilson, *Diderot* (New York: Oxford, 1972), 136-37.

Chief among the technological marvels of the musical world was the piano, an instrument that began to make its way at the beginning of the new era. Prior to that time, it had been a comparatively rare instrument, an occasional part of a collection made by music-loving nobles.[12] At first, the instrument seemed most used for accompanying singers and for solo performance in a chamber setting. By 1770, it had found its way into public concerts in London and Paris and had attracted builders to provide instruments for a newly-aroused public.[13] Over the next decades, the cultivators of the useful arts transformed it by more effective keyboards, actions, and hammers, by better strings and stringing dispositions, by iron frames capable of supporting the tension of the strings, by the mechanism of the sustaining pedal, and a host of other innovations.

In the process, the piano became a true solo instrument able to take its place as a partner in smaller ensembles or even compete with the full orchestra in concertos.[14] In this way, the keyboard instrument moved from public chambers for three to four hundred auditors—suitable for the harpsichord—to large concert halls; a promethean reaching out.

At the same time, entrepreneurs managed to create more compact models, well-built attractive pieces of furniture, which filled households with the rich sonority of new music. The piano could cover the complete pitch range of all the other instruments. It could control dynamics. It could accompany other instruments and the voice, play pieces composed specifically for it, and sample, through transcriptions, the whole of musical literature. Technology of a single instrument had transformed the musical world.

Inventors and artisans similarly transformed other instruments. Even the violin, fitted with a longer finger board placed at a sharper angle and played with a Tourte bow, gained power suitable for larger venues. The brass instruments, which had been limited to only parts of the scale, now acquired valves that allowed a complete chromatic scale. Makers such as Boehm and Buffet, reworked the flute and reed instruments to give them bigger tone and more reliable actions. Adolphe Sax invented a whole new family of instruments. Wieprecht filled out the brass choir with the tuba.

Technological advances brought new tonal ideals. The unique timbre of the newly favored piano came from the leather or felt used for its hammers and

---

[12]James Parakilas, *Piano Roles* (New Haven: Yale, 1999), 19-20.

[13]Arthur Loesser, *Men, Women and Pianos, A Social History* (New York: Simon and Schuster, 1954), 46.

[14]Loesser's pathbreaking social history *Men, Women and Pianos* has been supplemented by specialized studies and brought up to date in recent years by, among others: Parakilas, *Piano Roles*, (designed to cover "Three Hundred Years of Life with the Piano") and by Edwin M. Good, *Giraffes, Black Dragons, and other Pianos* (Stanford: Stanford University, 1982) which is "A Technological History from Cristofori to the Modern Concert Grand," a story told by detailed description of outstanding typical instruments.

from the different acoustic effects of a string struck rather than plucked. Loesser contrasted harpsichord and piano thus:

> A sharp, bright sound—a clear, well-defined, unambiguous statement of individual tone—such as the earlier eighteenth century had liked, was no longer wanted. The yearning was for a vague, mellow tone-cloud, full of ineffable promise and foreboding, carrying intimations of infinity.[15]

The harpsichord's primary function was as a continuo instrument. It provided

> rhythmic leadership and a harmonic framework for the rest of the ensemble. In fact the harpsichord was there for the other musicians more than for the audience, and its pinging notes were ideal for catching the ears of the other musicians spread out in the choir of a church, or in the pit and on the stage of an opera house, cutting through the rest of the music as well as the noise of the audience.[16]

Whereas the piano had a different function.

> Because the piano had the expressive powers that the harpsichord lacked, it could imitate the effects of the orchestra as a whole—largely the effects of massed string instruments—just as it could imitate the effects of the singers in an opera or a choir. But it would imitate them on its own terms, on its own intimate scale, in its own proper space. It would transport the rhetoric and drama of music making in the opera house or church into the private chamber.[17]

Even the other instruments, designed to become more reliably responsive and more naturally in tune, moved away from the distinctive elements that made for clear-cut lines in polyphony in favor of new ideals of blend and fusion. Manufacturers and musicians began to think of instruments as choirs of brass, choirs of woodwinds, and choirs of strings, from which could arise melodic voices that would retain touch with their tonal families.

To be properly termed promethean, technological advances, symbolized by the Titan's fire, had to reach out to "all mankind," a manifest impossibility if that meant each and every living person; yet the changes were so widespread that scarcely a person would not have been touched in some manner. In regard to the piano, we learn from an article in the *Revue et Gazette Musicale* of 1845, that

---

[15]Loesser, *Men, Women and Pianos,* 340.
[16]Parakilas, *Piano Roles,* 18-19.
[17]Parakilas, *Piano Roles,* 19.

a careful survey had established that there were 60,000 pianos in Paris, with about 100,000 persons who could play them. The city's million people might have been roughly, divided into 300,000 families—which meant that one family out of five, or twenty percent, possessed a piano and that one person in ten of the entire population could play it or at it.[18]

Originally an individual craftsman working with a few assistants might turn out about 19 pianos a year. Broadwood in early years (1782-1802) managed about 400 a year. By 1824, the firm could produce an annual average of about 1,680.[19] Later in the nineteenth century, production reached such heights that various firms[20] found it profitable to specialize in piano parts—felts, actions, frames, and cases—which could now be supplied to many makers who were relieved of the tasks of making an array of diverse items. Truly these were "going out" if not to all mankind, at least to great and growing numbers of an increasing populace.

Other instruments than the piano were necessary for large portions of the population. Demand ran high in civic and military groups. In 1838, Wieprecht brought together in Berlin sixteen infantry bands and sixteen cavalry bands, more than a thousand wind players and two hundred percussionists. By World War I, there were 541 bands in the Prussian military. Late in the nineteenth century, Berlin had about 100,000 people involved in bands, including a large number of civic bands in addition to the military ones.[21] The French Orphéon Society, begun in 1833 primarily to foster choral singing, began quickly adding bands to its projects. By the end of the nineteenth century, it had 1,711 Harmonies—bands, some with over one hundred players—plus four to five thousand Fanfares, more like drum and bugle corps.[22]

---

[18]Loesser, *Men, Women and Pianos,* 386.

[19]Loesser, *Men, Women and Pianos,* 234-35.

[20]Loesser, *Men, Women and Pianos,* 520-25. Good, *Giraffes,* 162-63, 178-80 in his sixth chapter on the technological changes made in France in the second and third decades of the nineteenth century, gives as much factual material on the use of steam power as can be amassed.

[21]David Whitwell, *The 19th Century Wind Band and Wind Ensemble in Western Europe,* The History and literature of the Wind Band and Wind Ensemble, vol. 5 (Northridge, Calif.: WINDS Box 513, 1983), 36, 46.

[22]The factual information on the Orphéon is given in Henri Maréchal and Gabriel Parès, *Monographie universelle de l'Orphéon, sociétés chorales, harmonies, fanfares, avec documents inédits, recueillis par les représentants de la France à l'étranger* (Paris: C. Delagrave, 1910). The relation of the Orphéon societies to prevailing theories of society is reported by Jane Fulcher, "The Orphéon Societies: 'Music for the workers' in Second-Empire France," *International Review of the Aesthetics and Sociology of Music* 10 (1979): 47-56. Neither study gives much material on the repertory or the love of music of the participants. Further information, by Eduard Hanslick, on the place of the Orphéons in society plus material, from various sources, on their instrumentation and repertoire is recorded in Whitwell, *19th Century Wind Band,* 171-79.

Despite the growing number of musicians and music lovers, the number was still small enough that instrument makers retained the craft tradition, a master and a workshop of apprentices who produced beautifully crafted instruments.[23] Makers did not, until near the middle or even the end of the era, take significant advantage of the power sources of the industrial revolution for the making of standardized factory instruments.

Among the other technological innovations transforming musical life, those of printers and publishers proved especially fruitful, perhaps more promethean in their use of technology and their modes of dissemination than the transformations wrought in instruments. Music printing had long been a complex operation since it required such a remarkable variety of signs. As the new style became established, those signs—phrasing, articulation, dynamics, accents, written descriptions of the feeling quality of the music—multiplied and made the task ever more difficult. The method of engraving gave beautiful results but required highly skilled workers who, of necessity, had to work rather slowly. Now the race was on to get new compositions out quickly and to large numbers of the populace.

Immanuel Breitkopf, capitalizing on the work of several others, developed a musical type that could be set and printed quickly. The most important breakthroughs came, however, first with the development of lithography and later with the use of offset printing. One has only to peruse the catalogues of Hofmeister to realize how the musical world of the new era became inundated with publications. A portion of this excess sprang from an advertising mindset designed to sell each wonder of the day with a maximum of profit. The publisher Schlesinger, for example, at the success of Donizetti's *La Favorita* in Paris asked the young Richard Wagner to make the following arrangements:

1) a complete arrangement of the opera for voice and piano
2) an arrangement of the whole work for piano solo
3) ditto for four hands
4) a complete arrangement for a quartet
5) ditto for two violins
6) ditto for cornet.[24]

[23]Professional musicians still choose individually crafted instruments. They are usually offered several and try them out before deciding. Among string players there is a constant, and expensive, quest for proven instruments by masters of the past. The numerous student players of brass or woodwinds usually are content with factory standardized instruments offered at affordable prices. This is similar to typewriters (when such were still in use); the speed champions performed on machines specially fabricated for them attaining feats that could not be duplicated on standard factory items.

[24]Ernest Newman, *The Life of Richard Wagner,* 4 vols. (New York: Knopf, 1933), I:290-91. Alexander Ringer, "Musical Taste and the Industrial Syndrome," *International Review of Aesthetics and Sociology of Music* 5 (1974), 145-47; reminds us that the law of supply and demand could sometimes corrupt high ideals.

Many publishers avoided this crass commercialism and reached the serious amateur—often those musically minded people enjoying evenings of family music. To this market came the piano transcriptions of symphonies and overtures for piano solo or piano duet; Volksausgabe—people's editions—of C. F. Peters that could be bound and stamped with the possessor's name; and bound editions of items such as Mendelssohn's *Lieder ohne Worte*, decorated on the cover with sprigs of leaves and flowers, and even a flute playing putto, the elegance giving an indication of esteem. So daunting is the task of gaining bibliographic control of the huge new repertory, that RISM, the Répertoire Internationale des Sources Musicales, has had to stop cataloguing shortly after the beginning of the nineteenth century.

Material advances in technology, such as those outlined above, grew exponentially, constantly reaching out to greater numbers of performers and auditors. Like the fire of Prometheus, they swept away the old and placed the new in the hands of an ever growing public.

3. The Proposal: The Second Main Theme

The second main theme is embedded in the story of how Prometheus took pity on suffering primitive men and women and gave them, through certain basic gifts, a command of their own education and control over their lives so that they might continually rise to higher realms. Prometheus's thoughts in the wilderness are interrupted by the appearance of the Oceanides, Oceanus's nurturing daughters, a group of barefoot girls with wings of sea birds. They, the great chorus of the tragedy, offer sympathy. They want to help him improve his lot. It is to them that he will offer his most private thoughts and knowledge. Oceanus arrives on a winged horse. As a brother Titan, he is trying to find a way to release Prometheus from his bonds. A sort of Polonius figure who speaks in maxims, he wants Prometheus to acknowledge his transgression and regain his favor with Zeus. He offers to intercede for him, but Prometheus, firm in his commitment as a benefactor of humanity, refuses and sends Oceanus away.

Prometheus turns to the Oceanides:

> hear,
> what wretched lives people used to lead,
> how babyish they were—until
> I gave them intelligence,
>   I made them
> masters of their own thought...[1]
>   for them I invented
>   NUMBER: wisdom
> Above all other.
>   And the painstaking putting together of
> LETTERS: to be their memory
> of everything, to be their Muses'
>   mother, their
>   handmaid![2]

He taught humanity matters of health, herding, cultivation of crops and the reading of signs. His making them "masters of their own thought" is nearly

[1]Aeschylus, *Prometheus Bound*, 49 (lines 630-35).
[2]Aeschylus, *Prometheus Bound*, 50 (lines 660-67).

Prometheus (Gravelot[3]),
*Iconologie par figures ou Traité
complet des allegories, em-blèmes,
&c. Ouvrage utile aux artistes,
aux amateurs, et peu-vent servir à
l'éducation des jeunes personnes,*
Plate 33 of volume IV (1791).

Here man is represented—
according to the accompanying
explanation—at the moment
when he is receiving "life and
feeling" from the Titan. It is a
moment of enlightenment as the
Titan's torch begins to illumine
the man who has been in
darkness or even without life.
Note especially that the work is
to be "useful for artists, for
amateurs, and can be used for *the
education of young people.* Such
figures were originally published
in the *Almanachs iconologiques,* a
series published between 1765
and 1781. One of the predominate ways of spreading education lay in periodicals—the
periodical symphonies, the poetic/musical almanacs, the serialized novels, and even in
this case a serial publication of icons.

Courtesy of Washington University Libraries, Department of Special Collections

identical to the "release from self-incurred tutelage," Kant's oft-quoted
description of the Enlightenment Period of the era after the Baroque. This
second main theme of the promethean myth is not as outwardly spectacular as
the theft of fire and its ability to foster technology. However, the gift of a
constantly evolving education for all peoples is equally important, perhaps even
more so (illustration above). Prometheus, the Forethinker, is one who sees and

[3]On the artist, Gravelot, see Gordon N. Ray's *The Art of the French Illustrated Book, 1700 to 1914* (New York:
Pierpont Morgan Library, 1982, 1986), 36-50 and Vera Salomons's *Gravelot* (London: Bumpus, 1911).

plans not just for the moment but for the future.[4] He would have mankind do likewise—as indeed the Prometheans did. Childhood education initiated by pioneers such as Oberlin and Pestalozzi gradually expanded into public schooling and literacy training for all, including women.

The tragedy ends after a harrowing scene with Io, daughter of Inachus, the river god. Zeus has turned her into a white heifer and Hera has set a gadfly upon her. Prometheus, seer of the future, tells Io that Zeus will eventually be overthrown by her son, Heracles. After Io leaves to pursue her sorrowful way, Hermes, messenger of Zeus, arrives to offer help if Prometheus will recant his actions for humanity. When Prometheus refuses, Hermes announces the punishment that will be his lot: the rocks around him will swallow him for a long period of time and when, at last, he sees the light again, the eagle of Zeus, a vulture,[5] will eat at his liver. Finally Prometheus and the Oceanides intone a great chant on the injustice of Zeus.[6]

The drama is so powerful that one can easily understand the fascination that it has had for many.[7] Its hope for a bright future gives it an added attraction for those seeking a better life. Prometheus combines the gift to transform earthly life in a material way *and* the intellectual insight to find values and meaning in that life through each newly endowed man and woman.

---

[4]The myth in its several versions is filled with various possible meanings. See Paul A. Bertagnolli's "Liszt, Goethe, and a Musical Cult of Prometheus," *Liszt and the Birth of Modern Europe,* Analecta Lisztiana III (Hillsdale, NY: Pendragon, 1998), 172-75.

[5]The Eagle is the symbol of Zeus. At one time Zeus had turned himself into an eagle in order to carry off Ganymede who became the god's lover and cup bearer. The word "eagle" by itself, however, does not portray its mission. Eagle is apt to connote today a heroic stance such as the American eagle, the eagle of Germany, or the Napoleonic eagle. In the play, Hermes speaks of "the winged hound of Zeus, the ravening eagle" (translation of Herbert Weir Smyth). I have opted to use the word "vulture," which in a single word conveys the purpose of the eagle. *Vautour,* as a word for the god's eagle, was frequently used in the promethean literature of the Enlightenment.

[6]The other plays in the trilogy, *Prometheus Unbound* and *Prometheus Fire-Carrier,* now exist only in fragments not sufficient to reconstruct their meaning so that we cannot be sure of Aeschylus's ultimate solution to the tragedy. The scholar C. J. Herington suggests only a general trend. "Above all, the fragments confirm the hypothesis that Prometheus's moments of solemn prophecy in the *Prometheus Bound* are to be accepted as describing what actually happened later in the trilogy. Prometheus was released in the end, and by Heracles, the descendant of Io. The episode of the Garland (fragments 15 through 17), so far as it can now be made out, suggests even that Prometheus's vision (*Bound* lines 282-283) of a spontaneous, mutual friendship between himself and Zeus was fulfilled. The general drift of the trilogy now becomes clear, also; it is a universal progress from confusion and torment, at all levels of the universe, toward peace and joy." [Aeschylus, *Prometheus Bound,* 16-17].

[7]Its role in literature has been traced in the magisterial work of Raymond Trousson, *Le Thème de Prométhée dans la littérature européenne* (Geneva: Droz, 1964). Several other versions than that of Aeschylus are known, especially one that makes Prometheus the creator of humankind; another version incorporates the Pandora myth and yet another includes his Titan brother, Epimetheus (After-Thinker). The main point of his service to humanity is in all versions.

(La Symphonie.)

The Symphony, L'*Illustration*, #128, Vol. V, Saturday, August 1, 1845, p. 381.

The symphony is portrayed on the Beethoven Monument (erected in Bonn in 1845) as an idealized woman, a symbol of the nobility of art. See also the similar figure by Gavarni in Jules Janin's *Les Symphonies de l'hiver* (Paris: Morizot, 1858).

Courtesy Wilson Library
Libraries of the University of Minnesota at Minneapolis

Composers, writers, and visual artists, no longer servants of the church or nobility, now seemed infused with the power of individual thought.[8] The new musician might still be called *maestro* [*maître* or *Meister*] in the traditional way but more and more he was given a name befitting his new-found status: *artist*, a word with a halo around it. Berlioz did not title his *Fantastic Symphony* "Episode in the Life of a Musician" nor did Schumann found the *Neue Zeitschrift für Musik* for "Musicians and Music Lovers." Both used the word "artist," a term that gave nobility to their craft, (illustration opposite page) the desire to rise above the shallow values of the commercial market, a hope not always realized.[9]

In German-speaking lands, the composer at times became the Tone Poet, the *Tondichter*, a term that combined the word for sound with that of poem— "sound" the very essence of music and "poem" in the Greek sense of a *creation*, something made in the grip of the *divine*. Music itself became known as "the divine art." The claim to be an artist rested, however, not solely on effusive or self-serving declarations, nor on honorific names. It arose as part of a larger outlook. The "artist" no longer practiced a craft but one of the "fine arts," arts exceeding mere practicality, something exalted above the useful arts.[10]

In 1746, the Abbé Charles Batteux put forth in his treatise *Les Beaux Arts réduits à un même principe*,[11] a schematic system for the arts of music, poetry, painting, sculpture, and dance. He grouped them all into a category of "fine arts," a concept still accepted today. These *beaux arts*, self sufficient in his view, were raised to a new level, an entity free of its former restraints as ornaments of

---

[8]Although at times they might have to sacrifice individual aspiration to financial security and commercial demand.

[9]Periodicals of the era addressed the amateur market in one degree or another. They carried notices and reviews of music and concerts, a necessary help in an age when so much music was being published and performed. Often they promoted local events and supported local pride though some journals had correspondents in a variety of European cities so that the musical devotee could be informed of the larger scene. Time and time again, musical affairs were paired with theatrical reports, sometimes paired with mode, fashion, and the social scene, yet again with businesses that wanted to promote their own publications. "Artist" represented an ideal, not always a reality.

[10]Jules Janin rhapsodizes thus: "What a fine word—artist! It is as if one said intelligent…he is one of the happy men of the world, a dreamer, a careless philosopher little disturbed by the material facts of life…a worthy man whose only cares are sound, color, tune, soul and heart" in "Etre artiste," opening essay in the first issue of *L'Artiste* (1831).

[11]Charles Batteux, *Les Beaux Arts réduits à un même principe* (Paris: Durand, 1746). This is also available in a reprint of 1970 by the Johnson Reprint Corporation as part of the series, *Classics in Art and Literary Criticism*, under the editorship of René Wellek. Paul Oskar Kristeller's "Modern System," *Journal of the History of Ideas* 11 (1951): 501-27; 12 (1952): 17-24, traces the emergence of Batteux's ideas and shows that the concept of the fine arts arose for the first time in mid-eighteenth century. An important follow-up to Kristeller's work is Georges Matoré's, "Les Notions d'art et d'artiste à l'époque romantique," *Revue des Sciences Humaines* 16 (1951): 120-37. Matoré's work has the added advantage of dating the first appearance of important terms. He introduces the important word *sentiment* into the discussion.

courtly life or backgrounds for religious observances. They were as free and open to humanity[12] as Prometheus had promised when he made humans "masters of their own thought."

Batteux went beyond his own basic principle of the "imitation of nature" when he approached the art of music. He knew that music entered the realm of feeling (*sentiment*), a quality that became one of the distinguishing marks of the new era. He realized that "the heart has its intelligence independent of words, and when it is touched everything is clearly understood."[13]

He had before him a lively theater culture in which the poetry, music, and choreography each played a part forming a "union of the arts."

> Thus when artists separate these three arts in order to cultivate and polish them with more care, each one in particular, they ought not to lose sight of the first order of nature nor think they can do without the others. They ought to be united, nature demands it, taste requires it.[14]

Even more boldly, he kept the place of honor for music, the art dependent upon feeling and sentiment.

> It is music alone that apparently has the right to unfold all its charms. The theater is for her. Poetry has only the second place and dance the third.[15]

To this union of the theatrical arts he added architecture, painting, and sculpture that "ought to prepare the locales and the scene of the spectacle and to do this in a manner corresponding to the dignity of the actors and the quality of the subjects at hand."[16] Here we have, in kernel, the power of drama and even something akin of the "complete art work," a hallmark of the Promethean Age. Batteux's concept of the fine arts spread rapidly. In 1751, Johann Adolf Schlegel translated the treatise into German.[17] Even more importantly, the concept formed the basis of Johann Georg Sulzer's monumental *Allgemeine Theorie der schönen Künste und Wissenschaften* (1771-74), a work in which music's place became so important that Sulzer had to draw upon musical experts to help him.

---

[12]The actual independence of the arts from the old patrons took place gradually and only gained momentum bit by bit throughout the Promethean Era.

[13]Batteux, *Beaux Arts*, 285-86.

[14]Batteux, *Beaux Arts*, 300.

[15]Batteux, *Beaux Arts*, 303.

[16]Batteux, *Beaux Arts*, 307.

[17]Under the title *Einschränkung der schönen Künste auf einen einzigen Gegensatz*. His elder brother, Johann Elias Schlegel, anticipated some of the principles of Batteux in his *Abhandlung von der Nachahmung* (1742-45).

The years around 1750 bristled with other grand projects, each endeavoring to understand and use knowledge as Prometheus would have it: man and the natural world, man and the world of work and technology. The first volume of the *Encyclopédie*, a Methodical Dictionary of Arts and Trades, appeared in 1751.[18] Jean Le Rond d'Alembert, in the preface, divided the whole realm of knowledge and understanding into those items based on (1) memory, (2) reason, and (3) imagination. Music, painting, sculpture, architecture and engraving found their place in the realm of "imagination" and all under the subdivision "poetry," thereby signifying their exalted place. As part of this larger outlook concerning the value of art—practiced by the noble artist—came philosophical speculation about art itself and its limits, an inquiry that became an established branch of philosophy called "aesthetics," using the title given to the work on sensory perception by Alexander Gottlieb Baumgarten in his *Aesthetica* of 1750-58. Almost simultaneous with this general recognition came an interpretation of a wilder type of expression that involved mystery, abnormality, and even terror—such things as the heroes and warfare of the imagined Celtic bard Ossian, the wilder scenes of Henry Fuseli,[19] or the avalanches and conflagrations of French rescue operas.[20] Edmund Burke in 1757 termed this "the sublime,"[21] one part of a duality in which the awe inspiring "sublime" was opposed to the "beautiful in form." The concept was discussed by several great thinkers of the age—Diderot, Lessing, Kant and Schiller—and the term "sublime" became widely accepted.[22]

---

[18]See Appendix A.

[19]A convenient source for the works of Fuseli is the exhibition catalogue, *Henry Fuseli, 1741-1825* (London: Tate Gallery, 1975). No. 78 in this catalogue is a sketch of Prometheus in which Fuseli has turned an academic exercise into an expressive theme. No. 73 is a pencil and watercolor sketch of the chaining of Prometheus. Recently two exhibitions have presented works in the tradition of the sublime: the exhibition of works of Girodet in Paris and at the Chicago Institute of Arts, and an exhibition centered on Fuseli and related artists at the Tate Britain in London. This latter presentation is accompanied by a splendid book of essays and colored plates: Martin Myrone, *Gothic Nightmares: Fuseli, Blake and the Romantic Imagination* (London: Tate Publishing, 2006). Special attention should be given to the essay "Perverse Classicism," pp. 53-99, which includes substantial discussion of Fuseli and his Prometheus images.

[20]Spectacular theater effects were not new. The Baroque Age cultivated the art of the theatrical machine and produced extraordinary stage productions in a genre often called the "marvelous." In the Promethean Era many of the effects were of natural phenomena, ordinary people, and historical situations—all of these related to the "human-centered" view of the time.

[21]Edmund Burke, *A Philosophical Enquiry into the Origins of our Ideas of the Sublime and the Beautiful* (London: R. and J. Dodsley, 1757). Burke's *Enquiry* is selected as a clear-cut exposition of what had been discussed previously by a number of English philosophers, Addison and Hume among them. The concept first appears in ancient Greece in a work by the so-called Longinus. See also Roger B. Larsson's "The Beautiful, the Sublime and the Picturesque in Eighteenth-Century Musical Thought in Britain" (Ph.D. diss., State University of New York at Buffalo, 1980).

[22]See Appendix B.

The artist became a standard bearer of the new era which brought to the wider audience an art that raised man to a higher state far beyond that brutish one in which the Forethinker had found him ages before and even beyond what had been accomplished in the intervening ages before 1750. In recognition, the artist became celebrated in festivals, in statues, in venerated tombs, in monuments, or portraits.[23]

Poet's Corner in Westminster Abbey, a series of monuments to literary artists—and including the musician, Händel—was so designated in the eighteenth century by Oliver Goldsmith, himself a friend and admirer of Burke. The Temple of British Worthies in the Elysian Fields in the gardens at Stowe was designed around 1735 to display busts of Pope, Milton, Shakespeare, Locke, Newton, Bacon and others.[24]

Le Parnasse François, a monument conceived by Titon du Tillet and sculpted in 1721 by Louis Garnier, is a bronze model of the Mount of Parnassus on which were displayed figures of the most illustrious poets and musicians of France—Racine, Corneille, Mlle. De Scudéry, La Fontaine, Segrais, Boileau, Lully and others. A colossal monument, based on the model, was to be erected in the center of Paris, a project which never came to pass.[25] The Panthéon in Paris was set aside in 1791 to keep the remains of those deserving of a nation's tribute. The cemetery of Père Lachaise likewise celebrates those "illustrious men and women who were born to no titles, but achieved fame by their own energy and their own genius...a nobler royalty—the royalty of heart and brain."[26]

In music, among numerous examples of tribute to the artist was the Beethoven statue at Bonn, a project which almost foundered in 1839 until Franz Liszt took it under his own protection. With his help, the statue was finally installed in August of 1845.[27] Yet more sweeping in honoring genius, the Weimar Court, the "Court of the Muses," in 1849 mounted a Goethe Festival[28] and inaugurated a statue, and then, in 1850, a Herder Festival to which Liszt

---

[23]In regard to tombs: a commoner's tomb in this age was frequently kept sacrosanct until only the bones were left; then they were removed and the space used for the next person. In regard to monuments, see Thomas Tolley's *Painting the Cannon's Roar: Music, the Visual Arts and the Rise of an Attentive Public in the Age of Haydn* (Aldershot: Ashgate, 2001), 182-85. In regard to portraits: prints of celebrities became collector's items for connoisseurs and publicity for aspiring musicians. Tolley, *Cannon's Roar*, 16, 164-65, 209-10. Heartz, in recognition of the essential role of visual art, includes a large number of illustrations and analyses of that art within his *European Capitals.*

[24]The entire issue of *Apollo* for June 19, 1973 is devoted to this monument.

[25]Judith Colton, *The Parnasse François: Titon du Tillet and the Origins of the Monument to Genius* (New Haven: Yale, 1979).

[26]Mark Twain, *The Innocents Abroad* (New York: New American Library, 1966), 101-02.

[27]Alan Walker, *Franz Liszt, The Virtuoso Years, 1811-1847,* rev. ed. (Ithaca: Cornell, 1987), 269-72, 417-26.

[28]Walker, *Franz Liszt, The Weimar Years, 1848-1861* (New York: Knopf, 1989) 119-21.

contributed incidental music for—a significant choice—Herder's *Der entfesselte Prometheus* (Prometheus Unbound).[29]

The social reformers used Prometheus as a congenial symbol. As early as the 1760s, the Chevalier de Jaucourt in his *Encyclopédie* article on Prometheus tied the Titan's struggle to that of the progressive thinkers of the Enlightenment. "The melancholy of leading a miserable life in a savage land where a vulture devours his liver, would that not be a vivid image of the depths and distressing meditations of a philosophe?"

One of the most widely read and influential treatments, a landmark in Romantic literature, was Shelley's *Prometheus Unbound* written between 1818 and 1820. Its idealistic appeal arose from his call to social action and from the beauty of his lyrics. With his poetic gifts he converted the myth into a musical image, the sound of the new society.

Then weave the web of the mystic measure;
From the depths of the sky and ends of the earth,
  Come, swift Spirits of might and of pleasure,
Fill the dance and the music of mirth,
  As the waves of a thousand streams rush by
To an ocean of splendour and harmony![30]

  And our singing shall build
  In the void's loose field
A world for the Spirit of Wisdom to wield:
  We will take our plan
  From the new world of man,
And our work shall be called the Promethean.[31]

The myth excited similar interest in the ranks of the more radical social reformers, those concerned with the material side of contemporary life. In his doctoral dissertation of 1841, Karl Marx, at the end of the introduction, called the Titan "the most eminent saint and martyr in the philosophical calendar."

---

[29]Walker, *Liszt, Weimar Years*, 121-23. The compositional and publishing history of Liszt's Prometheus music is extremely complex. See Paul Allen Bertagnolli's, "From Overture to Symphonic Poem, from Melodrama to Choral Cantata: Studies of the Sources for Franz Liszt's Prometheus and his Chöre zu Herders 'Entfesseltem Prometheus' " (Ph.D. diss., Washington University, St. Louis, 1998).

[30]Shelley, *Prometheus Unbound*, Act IV, Chorus of Spirits and Hours (lines 129-134).

[31]Shelley, *Prometheus Unbound*, Act IV, Chorus of Spirits (lines 153-58).

Marx himself was even portrayed in 1843 as Prometheus chained to the printing press of the *Rheinische Zeitung* with the Prussian Eagle gnawing at his liver.[32]

Prometheus, as presented by Aeschylus, did not anticipate a Utopia-to-Come—though some nineteenth-century social critics believed in such a possibility. Ideal communities they founded thrived for a time but did not survive. More realistic thinkers saw the gift of Prometheus in human terms, in the freedom to understand and to express themselves.

Goethe in his unfinished drama *Prometheus* (1774) recognized the gift to be neither completely joyous nor completely despairing. In a famous ode, the opening speech of a proposed third act—later set to music by Schubert[33] and Wolf—he had Prometheus proclaim:

Hier sitz' ich, forme Menschen	Here I sit, forming men
Nach meinem Bilde,	After my image,
Ein Geschlecht das mir gleich sei,	A race that will be like me,
Zu leiden, zu weinen,	To suffer, to weep,
Zu genießen und zu freuen sich,	To enjoy and be glad together,
Und dein nicht zu achten,	And to esteem you [Zeus] not at all,
Wie Ich.	Just as I.

What Prometheus gave was independence, to "strengthen Man in his own mind" as Byron put it.[34] From this recognition of what a human can achieve sprang the feeling of compassion, the understanding of the human condition. Love's joys and sorrows, the renewing forces of nature, the mystery of the night, the enchantment of childhood, the protest against tyranny and cruelty, in short, all that is human could take its place in the emotional world of the new age.

Our attitudes today have changed so radically that it is difficult for us to accept such promethean concepts as "progress" or "sentiment." At times our awareness of the dreary aspects of the era—the evils of the factory system, the

---

[32]Francis Wheen, *Karl Marx, A Life* (New York: Norton, 1999), figure 5 in an unpaginated and unnumbered series of illustrations. Prometheus became a prominent theme in the Soviet Union.

[33]Schubert set this poem for bass voice and piano in October of 1819 (D-674). He also set a cantata version of the Prometheus story (D-451) to the words of Philipp Dräxler von Carin; it was given in a private performance on 24 July 1816 and repeated in 1819 at the home of Ignaz von Sonnleithner. The music was lost during Schubert's lifetime and has never been found. The ode was also set by Hugo Wolf in 1889 for voice and piano and a few years later for voice with orchestral accompaniment.

[34]George Gordon Byron, "Prometheus," *The Complete Poetical Works*, vol. 4, ed. Jerome J. McGann (Oxford: Clarendon Press, 1986), 32.

excessive hours of labor, the usurpation of the democratic ideal by military and political forces, even the bathos of sentimentality—overwhelm us and lead us to abandon recognition of any positive qualities. Many of the contradictions of the era became evident as the twentieth century dawned. Some of the problems— intense nationalism, ecological damage, disparity between the "developed" world and the "undeveloped" and more—are still with us. Like all ages, it had its dark side. Yet nothing could stop the inexorable march of the new society within our focus on western Europe although not in portions of eastern Europe that retained a semi-feudal society during the era.

If one judges, however, by the life of the time preceding and the age afterward—neither of them golden ages—this era can be viewed in an affirmative manner, an aspiring age, the way in which Herder saw it when he proclaimed: "Use the fire that Prometheus brought to you, use it for yourselves. Let it shine brighter and more beautiful; it is the flame of the ever-progressing culture of man."[35]

---

[35]Johann Gottfried Herder, "Der entfesselte Prometheus, Scenen," *Sämtliche Werke,* vol. 4, ed. Bernhard Suphan and Carl Redlich (Berlin: Weidmann, 1884), 328. Herder had pondered, during a lifetime of literary work, the Prometheus myth.

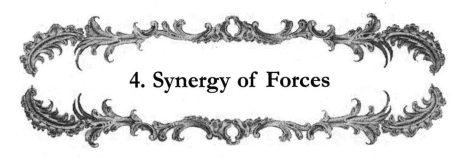

4. Synergy of Forces

The two promethean themes—so far presented separately—cannot be fully appreciated in isolation; they are intertwined. In tandem with the remarkable increase in manufacture of instruments, for instance, came the necessity of teaching large numbers of people both the fundamentals of music and the techniques of their chosen instruments.

The statement "large numbers of people" is not casual; it requires explanation. While the new public is often described as middle class or bourgeois, those terms, while essential, can be difficult or misleading if used as the sole criterion.[1] It was a time—if we consider the entire age—that witnessed in *western* Europe a movement of people from farm to city, to factory life, to wage-earners life, to merchant life, or even to executive life. The new broader arts public consisted of a mixed group that included some of the nobility, some of the merchants and their families, some of the professional musicians, some of the amateurs belonging to choirs or bands, and some of the citified folk who found means for occasional attendance at musical events—a mixture that grew more varied as the era unfolded and audiences experienced presentations going from the lighter fare of the pleasure gardens to the upper class subscription concerts attended by the members of a society of performers, directors, and auditors.[2]

Not only were there more people who could afford to follow and enjoy the arts; indeed, there were more and more actual persons within western Europe. Carl L. Becker presents a telling summary when he writes,

In 1685 the population of England was about 5,000,000. For centuries the increase had been so slight that Gregory King, an economist living in the early eighteenth century, estimated that there would not be 11,000,000 in England until the year 2300. But in fact there were 11,000,000 in England in 1815. In 1910, there were 36,900,000. Between 1801 and 1910 the population of France increased from about 25,000,000 to 39,000,000; during the same period the population in the

---

[1]William Weber, "The Muddle of the Middle Classes," *19th Century Music* 3/2 (1979), 175-85, outlines some of the problems that social historians have found in this usage. In any case, overwhelming numbers of peasants, quite removed from cultivated music circles, remained numerically the backbone of the various countries.

[2]Henry Raynor, *Music & Society Since 1815* (New York: Schoken, 1976), Chap. 7, offers a resumé of concerts both light and serious.

A vocal concert of the Orphéon Society in the National Circus on the Champs-Élysées in Paris, 1847, *L'Illustration* #215, Vol. IX, Saturday, March 27, 1847, p. 57, showing the large audiences at a later stage of the Promethean Age.

Courtesy Wilson Library,
Libraries of the University of Minnesota at Minneapolis

territories included in the German Empire of 1871 increased from 24,000,000 to 65,000,000. Nothing like this rapid increase had been known before.[3]

The principal reasons for this upsurge were the improvements in sanitation and medical treatment together with a decline in infant mortality—truly promethean changes.[4]

A new type of relationship between music producers and music consumers emerged, a type of "business" arrangement. It was dependent upon widespread listening experience and musical education. In the common schools the ordinary

[3]Carl L. Becker, *Modern History, The Rise of a Democratic, Scientific, and Industrialized Civilization* (New York: Silver Burdett, 1942), 502.
[4]This topic and its medical aspects are treated by Gay, *The Enlightenment*, 21-23.

person could find at least singing of folk songs and, often, some instruction in music reading. Solfège, Tonic Sol-Fa and Rousseau's number system became accepted methods of teaching note reading.[5]

During the Baroque Era, aspiring music students planning a professional career had found individual masters, teachers in the Italian conservatories, and the musicians of the various choir schools to instruct them. The establishment of the Parisian Conservatoire National de Musique et de Déclamation in 1795, once past its military and revolutionary stage, marked a turning point. The French government began subsidizing the training of talented students, the first step in what was to become for various countries a system of state-sponsored conservatories that spread musical culture throughout Europe. Outstanding teacher-musicians and directors often wrote textbooks, composed instructional manuals and études, set up tests for their students, and, in some cases even influenced music in the public schools.

Musical literacy served well the civic groups: the Männerchöre and Frauenchöre of Germany, the Caveau and Orphéon in France, and the festival choruses of England. Percy Scholes calls the nineteenth-century English cultivation of sight-singing a "mania (and mania is not too strong a word)."[6] Mania though it might be, the ability to read music opened new realms to the ordinary person in the same way that newspapers and magazines were giving the working classes a knowledge of worlds far beyond the village or the factory[7] while novels—such as those by Charles Dickens or George Sand—often published in magazines and newspapers, gave them a broader view of society, such as the difficult position of women or the cruelties visited upon the young and the poor.

A growing number of methods and studies testifies further to the great educational wave engulfing western Europe. The following table shows the most important keyboard texts for the Early Promethean Period.[8]

[5]Among the items in the vast literature on music education, prominent mention should be given to the numerous volumes edited and reprinted through the activity of Bernarr Rainbow under the general rubric of "Classic Texts in Music Education." While these lean heavily toward British sources, there are some from the continent as well. They include Rousseau's work on music reading as well as Joseph Mainzer's *Singing for the Million;* Mainzer, a disciple of song and note reading worked in Germany, France, and England.

[6]Percy A. Scholes, *The Mirror of Music*, 2 vols. (London: Novello and Oxford University, 1947), 1:3. The first chapter, entitled "The Sight-Singing Century," contains a listing of choral organizations, many dating from the eighteenth century.

[7]See Jonathan Rose, *The Intellectual Life of the British Working Classes* (New Haven: Yale University, 2001), 25. Rose gives enough facts to support the conclusion of Marshall McLuhan that "Print carries the individuating power of the phonetic alphabet much further than manuscript culture could ever do. Print is the technology of individualism" (*Gutenberg Galaxy: The Making of Typographic Man* [Toronto: University of Toronto, 1962], 158).

[8]The table shows primarily chronology but also the gradual change from methods for harpsichord or clavichord to those for the pianoforte, and also it shows the gradual appearance of methods designed specifically for beginners and for children. In addition to the methods of the (cont.)

STUDIES AND METHODS

1749	Humanus, P.C. (P. C. Hartung)	*Musicus theoretico-practicus*, Nürnberg The Theoretico-Practical Musician, "Part II containing a Methodical Guide to the Clavier that expounds a convenient, speedy, artful, and artful-appearing application of the fingers"
1750	Marpurg, F. W.	*Die Kunst das Clavier zu spielen*, Berlin Second volume issued in 1751, French translation 1755, Enlarged 1762
1753	Bach, C. P. E.	*Versuch über die wahre Art das Clavier zu spielen*, Berlin Part One, also 1859, Part Two issued in 1762, the whole reissued 1780 and 1797. This was followed by 6 Probe Sonatas and was later supplemented with 6 Easy Sonatinas. In addition, Emanuel Bach published various Easy Sonatas, Sonatas for the Ladies, and between 1779 and 1787, six collections of Sonatas, Rondos and Fantasies for Professionals and Amateurs
1753	Corrette, M.	*Le Maître de clavecin...méthode théorique et practique*, Paris
1755	Marpurg, F. W.	*Anleitung zum Clavierspielen*, Berlin Second edition in 1765, French translation 1756, Dutch translation 1760
1755	Königsperger, M.	*Der Wohlunterwissene Clavierschuler*, Augsberg
c. 1760	Pasquali, N. ,	*The Art of Fingering the Harpsichord*, London
1762	Kirnberger, J. P.	*Clavierübungen mit der Bachischen Applicator, in einer Folge von den leichtesten bis zu den schwersten Stücken* Keyboard exercises with the C.P.E. Bach fingering arranged according to the easiest to the most difficult pieces.
1765	Wiedeburg, M. J. F.	*Der sich selbst informirenden Clavier-Spieler* (3 parts, other volumes in 1767, 1775)
1765	Löhlein, G. S.	*Clavier-Schule*, Leipzig and Züllichau Second part 1781, this continued through various editions for nearly a century
c. 1766	Heck, J. C.	*The Art of Fingering*, London Second edition, c. 1780
1767	Petri, J. .S.	*Anleitung zur practischen Musik vor neu angehende Sänger und Instrumentenspieler*, Laubon Revised 1782
c. 1770	Heck, J. C.	*The Art of Playing the Harpsichord*, London
1771	Diderot, D.	*Leçons de clavecin et principes d'harmonie*, Paris Published under name of Anton Bemetzrieder

1779	Riegler, F. X.	*Anleitung zum Clavier für musikalische Lehrstunden,* Vienna Reissued 1791
1781	Schmidtchen	*Kurzgefassste Anfangsgründe auf das Clavier für Anfänger,* Leipzig
1782	Kobrich, J. J. A. B.	*Gründliche Clavierschule durchgehends mit praktischen Beyspielen erkläret,* Augsburg
1782	Merbach, G. F.	*Clavierschule für Kinder,* Leipzig
1783	Wolf, G. F.	*Kurzer aber deutlicher Unterricht in Klavierspielen,* Göttingen Also 1784, 1789, 1799
1784	Kauer, F.	*Kurzgefasste Clavierschule für Anfänger,* Vienna
c. 1785	Hook, J.	*Guida di musica;* being a complete book of instructions for beginners on the harpsichord or piano-forte, entirely on a new plan, calculated to save a great deal of time & trouble both to master & scholar. To which is added twenty-four progressive lessons in various keys, with the fingering marked throughout. Op. 37 Second Part, Op. 75 in 1794, *New Guide,* Op. 81 in 1796
1786	Bach, J. C. and Ricci, F. P.	*Méthode ou Recueil des connoissances élémentaires pour le Forte-Piano ou Clavecin. Oeuvre mêlée de Théorique et de Pratique*
1789	Türk, D. G.	*Klavierschule, oder Anweisung zum Klavierspielen für Lehrer und Lernende,* Leipzig and Halle
1790	Rellstab, J. C. F.	*Rellstabs Anleitung für Clavierspieler, den Gebrauch der Bachschen Fingersetzung, die Manieren und den Vortrag betreffend,* Berlin
1791	Nagel, J. F.	*Kurze Anweisung zum Klavierspielen, für Lehrer und Lernende,* Halle
1791	Chauvet l'aîne, G.	*Principes de musique pour le piano,* Paris
1796	Hüllmandel, N. J.	*Principles of Music chiefly calculated for the piano forte or harpsichord with progressive lessons,* Op. 12, London
1796	Dussek, J. L. & Pleyel, I.	*Instructions on the art of playing the pianoforte or harpsichord,* London, also in French in 1797 with principles of fingering and tuning
1796	Hering, C. G.	*Praktisches Handbuch zur leichten Erlernung des Klavierspielens für Lehrer und Lernende,* Halberstadt
1797	Milchmeyer, J. P.	*Die wahre Art das Pianoforte zu spielen,* Dresden
1798	Vogler, G. J.	*Claver-schola med 44 graverde tabellern,* Stockholm

Some columns of the catalogue of the publishing house of La Chevardière, printed within the score of Adolph Blaise's, *Annette et Lubin*, (1765).

La Chevardière realized the advertising value of such a catalogue inserted in his musical scores, a practice that persists even today. This particular publication printed 14 sections of his catalogue of vocal and instrumental music. Sometimes on title pages, he included addresses outside of Paris—Versailles and Lyons—where his publications could be purchased. He also published various arrangements and "popular" collections of airs, minuets and contradances as a means of delighting customers.

Courtesy of The Newberry Library

There were similar publications for the other instruments such as Geminiani's *Art of Playing on the Violin* (1752), Leopold Mozart's *Versuch einer gründlichen Violinschule* (1756), or Abbé le fils's *Principes du violon* (1761), although they were not as numerous as those for the keyboard.[9]

These tutors could be used to learn without a master[10] as, for instance, Adolph Bernhard Marx did with Daniel Gottlob Türk's *Clavierschule*.[11] They were meant, however, as their titles indicate, "for teachers and students." The profession of "music teacher" blossomed until it became an occupation[12] by itself as it did for Türk, Hering, and others. In large cities a significant number of such teachers were available; in Paris of 1783, for instance, there were 149 teachers of harpsichord and forte piano.[13]

Alongside the performance organizations, the ranks of learners and teachers, and the methods of teaching musical literacy, came the business enterprises.[14] These ventures used the new technologies of manufacturing and printing—and the blossoming device of advertising—in the service of education and financial profit (illustration opposite page).

Promethean Era, the era can justifiably be called the age of the étude, the technical study designed to help an aspirant master a particular difficulty of execution. In many cases, these technical studies—ranging from works for children up to the professional studies designed by the teachers of the Paris Conservatoire—began to incorporate *expressive character*. Even Türk's small pieces for children devoted to a particular aspect of nomenclature or technique frequently are given characteristic titles. At a later date, the Chopin Etudes acquired popular descriptive titles such as "Winter Wind" or "Revolutionary." These examples support the basic thesis of this essay: that the expressive ideal of the age encompassed both 1) clear, accessible construction and 2) character often expressed in dramatic ways.

[9]Still other publications of studies such as Locatelli's *L'Arte del violino*, Guillemain's *Amusement*, and works of Viotti and Tartini took revered places in the teaching repertory.

[10]The notation in these works and in printed music also gradually abandoned the older movable clefs in favor of the two principal clefs in use today. For reading of music the simplified solfège systems were favored. See Philippe Lescat's, "Réflexions sur l'éducation musicale en France au XVIIIe siècle," *L'Éducation musicale en France*, ed. Danièle Pistone (Paris: Presse de l'Université de Paris-Sorbonne, 1983): 28-31.

[11]Marx later studied basso continuo with Türk himself. See the article on Marx by Birgitte Moyer in the *New Grove Dictionary of Music and Musicians*, 1980 ed.

[12]Michael Roske, "The Professionalism of Private Music Teaching in the 19th Century: A study with social statistics," *Council for Research in Music Education Bulletin USA* 91 (spring 1987): 143-48, is an attempt to reconstruct such an occupation in Altona (part of Hamburg today) in the first half of the 19th century.

[13]Tome I, Étude Historique, of Barry Brook's *La Symphonie Française dans la seconde moitié du XVIIIe siècle* (Paris: Institut de Musicologie de l'Université de Paris, 1962), 25; Philippe Lescat, "Réflexions," 26.

[14]William Weber, "Mass Culture and the Reshaping of European Musical Taste, 1770-1870," *International Review of Aesthetics and Sociology of Music* 7 (June 1977): 6-12, considers the change from the "personalized commerce" of the early years of the era and the "merchandizing" of the later years.

Publishers could prime this market still further with music journals to meet the requirements of a wide clientele—amateurs and professionals alike. Imogen Fellerer has recorded something over 1,200 periodicals begun during the time period and the locale we are considering.[15] As we move into the Middle Promethean Period (1800-1850), the public now had newspapers available and more people literate enough to read them. The newspaper editors found that they could interest people with musical reviews and articles. Readers, in turn, as they became involved with the art, asked for more coverage in the newspapers or in the journals. With such synergy of forces a "music business" was established.

Literacy grew not only by the written word but also by visual illustration. The *Encyclopédie* enhanced its teaching a thousand fold by eleven volumes of magnificently-drawn plates. Books of the age seemed incomplete without illustrations, vignettes, full-page plates, headpieces and tailpieces. In the hands of an accomplished artist, a book could become a treasured artwork in itself, an item to be collected for its artistic quality.[16]

The ancient art of drawing now took on the dimensions of a trade—the making and marketing of engravings, etchings, or illustrations by related techniques. Artists made copies of famous art works, freshly conceived subjects, and portraits of noted people—composers, artists, and statesmen. Such prints became objects of display and esteem, constant reminders of what could be accomplished in the Promethean Age. Rousseau had such a collection; so did Haydn.[17] At least one important music dealer, Artaria of Vienna, began his trade as a dealer in prints, "relatively inexpensive works of art intended for a broad public."[18] Eventually the house became a world leader in art works and maps.

A person who wanted an art work but could not afford a painting turned to the market of prints (illustration opposite page).

Not only were prints in demand but busts of famous figures, frequently executed in plaster or terracotta, were collected. In the case of Houdon, this was turned into a business.[19]

Houdon was the first modern sculptor who did not hesitate to mass produce his sculptures or to delegate production to his workshop. In this he far surpassed

---

[15]In her article "Periodicals" in *The New Grove Dictionary of Music and Musicians* as well as in her earlier work, *Verzeichnis der Musikzeitschriften des 19. Jahrhunderts* (Regensburg: G. Bosse, 1986).

[16]Gordon N. Ray, *The Art of the French Illustrated Book, 1700 to 1914* (New York: Dover, 1986) and *The Illustrator and the Book in England from 1790 to 1914* (New York: Dover, 1991) both based on earlier editions by the Pierpont Morgan Library, contain examples, history, and bibliography of this complex subject.

[17]Tolley, *Cannon's Roar*, 324-27 lists Haydn's collection.

[18]Tolley, *Cannon's Roar*, 95.

[19]Haydn had five busts of himself; Tolley, *Cannon's Roar*, 326-27. Considering his success in setting "Let there be light," we might also note that his collection included an "Apollo," god of light, in alabaster.

A pastoral scene after Claude Lorrain

This image is part of a series of prints issued c. 1776 by John Boydell, print seller to England and the continent; a landscape with cattle and goats (whose placid nature made them favorites of Claude). The erect figure, Hermes (Mercury) can be recognized by the wings on his heels, his broad brimmed hat, the petasus, and his messenger wand, the caduceus. The figure seated by the tree is a shepherd. By his portrayal as a fair youth, he might possibly be interpreted as Apollo though he carries no symbols of that god of light. Hermes is portrayed as an adult. On the first day of his life he had stolen Apollo's herd of cattle and also had killed a turtle whose shell became a support for a new instrument, the lyre, which Hermes played, creating "a tumult...joyous and wild and wanton" according to Shelley's translation of Homer's *Hymn to Mercury*. Hermes later gave the lyre to Apollo. Then Apollo "with the plectrum strook the chords, and from beneath his hands a crash of mighty sounds rushed up, whose music shook the soul with sweetness, and like an adept his sweeter voice a just accordance kept" as Shelley puts it.

Courtesy a private collector

Caffieri, though the latter inundated academic institutions with various castings of his works. In fact, one scholar [François Souchal] has described Houdon's studio as a "veritable factory."[20]

The pace of these interactions between the arts and business constantly quickened. The industrial revolution, often symbolized as promethean, started with a "take-off point" which gradually developed into a period of "self-sustained growth."[21] Western Europe became more and more an entity in which the latest ideas and methods flowed rapidly from place to place. The *Correspondance Littéraire*, handwritten reports from Paris of the latest fashions, arts, and thought, circulated to the courts. Books and music of the publishing houses of Paris and London, became available at the great fairs, at the houses themselves, and also at the merchants who stocked the works of many publishers.[22] Finally, the railways catapulted Europe into a new milieu.[23] Thus was created a vast interaction, a synergy of forces, a new culture.

[20]Guilhem Scharf, "Houdon, 'Above All Modern Artists'," *Jean-Antoine Houdon — Sculptor of the Enlightenment* (Washington D.C.: National Gallery of Art, 2003), 22.

[21]Hobsbawm, *Age of Revolution*, 45, uses this metaphor and the one of being "airborne" for the year 1780.

[22]Sarah Adams, "International Dissemination of Printed Music During the Second Half of the Eighteenth Century," *The Dissemination of Music, Studies in the History of Music Publishing*, ed. Hans Lenneberg (Amsterdam: Gordon and Breach, 1994), 21-42. Adams has amassed a trove of materials, difficult to find, that indicate a whole network of dealers even before the publishing surge of the nineteenth century. Further information is found in Hans Lenneberg, *On the Publishing and Dissemination of Music, 1500-1850* (Hillsdale NY: Pendragon Press, 2003), 86-90 and Alec Hyatt King, "Music Circulating Libraries in Britain," *Musical Times* 119: 124-38.

[23]William Newman's *Sonata in the Classic Era*, 64, shows how dependent musicians were on travel and correspondence.

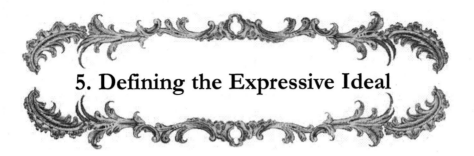

5. Defining the Expressive Ideal

One must, in seeking this ideal, consider the principal technical feature of promethean music: *a melodic orientation expressed in organized syntax of phrase and period.* These units combined into larger entities making a structure called "form,"[1] whose sections were identified by their melodic themes and thematic groups—set off by transitional passages of non-melodies—and by their tonalities, extended areas or planes of tonality.

Melodic themes had regularity and appealed through simplicity and directness; yet, such themes were considered not completely adequate if they lacked *expression.*[2] As Batteux put forth his ideas of the fine arts— including the high place he gave to music—he particularly inveighed against "calculated and geometric music"[3] and concluded that the "worst kind of musics are those that have no character."[4] Here is a key element of the new style. Our statement of the expressive ideal[5] can then be modified as: *music of melodic orientation expressed in organized syntax of phrase and period linked to the expression of character.*

Character became a dominant, all-pervasive goal not only in music but in all the fine arts of the Promethean Era. In the literary arts of the seventeenth and eighteenth-century, depictions of character and personality became the rage. According to J. W. Smeed,[6] the principal researcher, English *Characters* frequently had a witty quality, French *Characters* were tinged with features of the

---

[1]Baroque music generally did not attain "form" according to this conception; it relied on "procedure." The musicians of the Promethean Era developed phrase and period structure several decades before these units were identified by theorists. That type of melodic writing can be traced to the opera composers of the Neapolitan School starting with Vinci. See Heartz's *Music in European Capitals,* 101-03. This style of melody was codified by Heinrich Christoph Koch in *Versuch einer Anleitung zur Composition* 3 vols. (Leipzig: Böhme, 1782, 1787, 1793) and Anton Reicha, *Traité de mélodie* (Paris, 1814). Each viewed the smaller units united into a larger "form" called *Tonstück* by Koch, *Coupe* by Reicha.

[2]See Appendix C.

[3]Batteux, *Beaux Arts,* 286.

[4]Batteux, *Beaux Arts,* 282.

[5]Heartz, *Music in European Capitals,* 101, quotes Jean-Francois Marmontel, *Essai sur les révolutions de la musique en* France (1777): "Melody without expression is a small thing; expression without melody is something, but not enough. Expression and melody, both to the highest degree, where they can soar together: there is music's problem."

[6]J. W. Smeed, *The Theophrastan 'Character'* (Oxford: Clarendon Press, 1985).

contemporary portrait, whereas German *Characters* took on a didactic tone suitable to the moral weeklies in which they were published.[7]

In the visual arts, painters, such as the portrait and genre virtuoso, Jean-Baptiste Greuze, gained eminence through their portrayal of personal feelings not only in formal portraits but more particularly in personages of genre scenes. His figure of an old woman—used in several works—captures *character*.

> Her eyes are intently focused, her nostrils flared, her mouth open in an expression of anticipation or concern. The eccentric light source catches her face and left breast. Her clothes are mainly black and white, with some heavy impasto on her blouse and face: her rich reddish-brown hair is gathered in a spotted damson scarf.[8]

Sculptors, such as the virtuoso Jean-Antoine Houdon, succeeded in capturing the hair, the eyes, the skin tone, and above all, the attitude that showed the sitter's personality, profession, and energy, in short *"character."*[9] Among his large gallery of portraits is one of Gluck, without a wig, with pock-marked skin, an open shirt signifying the industry of the artist, and an uplifted face that suggests the seeker after operatic veracity. The sculptor defined his aims thus:

> One of the most beautiful attributes of the difficult art of statuary is that it preserves forms in all their truth and renders almost imperishable the images of men who have brought their nation glory or happiness. That idea has followed me constantly and encouraged me in my long labors.[10]

In the theatrical arts, authors thought that character should become the very heart of their plays. The *Encyclopédie* defined "character in individuals that a dramatic poet introduced on the stage" as:

> the propensity of the dominant passion that bursts out in all the bearing and speech of those individuals, that which is the principal and prime mover of all their actions, for example, ambition in Caesar, jealousy in Hermione, integrity in Burrhus, avarice in Harpagon, hypocrisy in Tartuffe, etc.

Character even acquired a meaning beyond its reference to the individual. At times, it was thought that it could contribute to the humanitarian ideals of the community. The philosophe, Diderot, believed that character and sensibility

---

[7] All stemmed from a work of Aristotle's follower, Theophrastus, *The Characters*—first published in the sixteenth century—as well as from certain teaching traditions, and other literary customs of the various countries according to Smeed.

[8] James Thompson, "Jean-Baptiste Greuze," *The Metropolitan Museum of Art Bulletin*, 47/3, 24.

[9] Andrew Butterfield, "Capturing Character," *The New York Review of Books*, 17 July 2003, 7-10.

[10] A handwritten note by Houdon cited by Guilhem Scherf, "Houdon, 'Above all Modern Artists'," *Jean-Antoine Houdon, Sculptor of the Enlightenment*, 17.

in the arts should not exist in isolation but should lead to civic good. He exclaimed, "Oh! What good would redound to men if all the imitative arts would adopt a common purpose and one day co-operate with the laws in making us love virtue and hate vice."[11] Character and humanity became more prized than noble birth. The Salieri/Beaumarchais opera, *Tarare* (1787) concludes with this phrase: "Mortals, whoever you might be, Prince, Priest, or Soldier—Man! Your grandeur on earth is not due to your rank, it is due completely to your character."[12]

Music's power of moving human feelings became a force in portraying the emotions which underly character.[13] That power sprang from music's own elements—(1) the tension or relaxation aspects of high and low pitches, of diatonic or chromatic movement, and of concordant or dissonant harmony plus (2) the feeling of movement stemming from the varieties of meter and rhythm. Music lacked some of the objective qualities of the other arts: words, objects, or material items. Artists however did not succeed by objective means. They exerted their most powerful effects only when the material objects they manipulated were arranged so as to arouse human feeling. Artists dealt with metaphor, attitude, gesture, contrast—artistic means connecting to the emotional world of mankind. Music might have limited power to "paint" objects but had the basic power of *sentiment* itself.

The French, lovers of music and dance allied to dramatic action, found it quite natural to speculate about musical character based on the arousal of specific emotions. Most of their musical theories sprang from speech and gesture, basic elements of natural human expression as well as of the theater.[14]

Batteux in his influential treatise maintained that, while speech, as a means for expression of ideas, is given much attention, truly voice and gesture are more natural and everywhere more commonly used—the "dictionary of simple Nature," they "reach the heart directly with no detour."[15] And so with music. His words are worth quoting again.

[11]Arthur M. Wilson, *Diderot* (New York: Oxford, 1972), 331, quoting a passage in Diderot's *Discours sur la poésie dramatique*.

[12]In the concluding moments of the opera, in a passage marked *lent et majestueux*, Nature and the Genius of Fire (identified as the sun) sing: "Homme! Ta grandeur sur la terre n'appartient point à ton état, elle est toute à ton caractère." *Tarare* has many of the qualities of the old lyric tragedy as John A. Rice notes in *The New Grove Dictionary of Opera*, but it is also a rescue opera in which the heroine is rescued from her incarceration in a harem of the wicked king.

[13]For many years, following the basic work on emotion in the nineteenth century by Charles Darwin and William James, psychology devoted little time to the study of emotion. In the last several decades that science has returned to the topic with some interesting results. Robert Tallant Laudon's article, "The Elements of Expression in Music: A Psychological Viewpoint" appears in the December 2006 edition of *The International Review of Aesthetics and Sociology of Music*.

[14]Consider Condillac's linking of language to gesture, *langage d'action*; Rousseau's linking of song and poetry, *langue des poètes*; and Diderot's fusion of language and feeling, *langue du coeur*.

[15]Batteux, *Beaux Arts*, 254-55.

On voit jufqu'au fond de ton   Onde,
On lit jufqu'au fond de mon cœur.

Le Ruisseau, Benjamin La Borde's *Choix de Chansons mises en musique* (first
edition, 1772-1775; second edition 1881)

Courtesy Music Library, University of Minnesota at Minneapolis

The worst kind of musics are those that have no character. There is not a sound in that art but what has its model in Nature and which ought to be, at least, a beginning of expression just as a letter or a syllable in speech.[16]

A "calculated and geometric music" would be like a prism that produces pretty colors but no picture.[17]

Some of the songbooks reveal not only through music but through illustration the character and nature of the persons of the song.

Moreau le jeune illustrated La Borde's *Choix de Chansons mises en musique* (1772-1775).[18] One plate for the song, *Le Ruisseau* shows the ubiquitous young man, shaded by a tree, gazing into the brook (illustration opposite page).

On voit jusqu'au fond de ton Onde,	One gazes into the depths of your water,
On lit jusqu'au fond de mon coeur.	One reads there the depths of my heart.

The text of the song is:

Ruisseau qui baigne cette plaine	Brook which bathes these fields
Je te ressemble en bien des traits	I resemble many of your features,
Ton jour même penchant t'entraine	Your life slips away
Le mien ne changera jamais,	Mine will never change,
Ton murmure flatteur et tendre	Your caressing and tender murmur
Ne cause ni bruit ni fracas,	Causes neither noise nor fuss,
Plein du souci qu'amour fait prendre	Full of cares caused by love
Si j'en murmure c'est tout bas.	My murmur is but a whisper.

The *galant homme* saw himself reflected in nature; he sang of nature and the human heart. In our hasty age when even the most private physical matters

---

[16]Batteux, *Beaux Arts,* 282.

[17]Batteux, *Beaux Arts,* 286. Pluche judged sonatas and many other musical types as being "to music as marbling is to painting." (VII, 116).

[18]It is generally conceded that La Borde is at best only marginally successful in conveying the spirit of the words, probably not as successful as Moreau was in his visual interpretations. Yet we must remember that La Borde was attempting something quite new, veritable first steps. Gordon N. Ray in *The Art of the French Illustrated Book 1700 to 1914* (Mineola, N.Y.: Dover, 1986), 91, states the difficulty for the illustrator: "Moreau's problem in dealing with La Borde's vapid, not to say nebulous, songs was considerable. They are so lacking in content that they rarely offer a narrative point for illustration. His solution was to create an idealized world, extending from the countryside to the city, in which all the actors are agreeable, and every scene is entrancing. The absence of constraint from La Borde's text was thereby converted into a positive advantage."

are allowed to "hang out," it is very difficult to appreciate these delicate romantic yearnings. Yet they constituted a revolution in feeling from the Baroque Era, an age which had exalted the regal and imperial but which was succeeded by an age in which the poet and musician, in search of character, dared to speak of gentleness, of fond affection.[19]

The opposite end of the spectrum, the sublime, could be found as well. Even the suicidal gunshot of Werther could be depicted in a keyboard accompaniment.[20] The Erlking and his haunting pursuit attracted composers. The most extreme wild and disordered phenomena were depicted in the theater. They reached a peak not only in the operas of the revolutionary decade but in the "grand operas" of the nineteenth century. Catastrophes were all the more powerful because they arose out of injustice and were resolved in favor of humanity, peace, and justice.[21] At the very least, they shocked and aroused an audience. They played to the new-found sense of humanity.

Still further intensity came when musical artists, in their new-found freedom, began to depict rapidly changing character evoking dramatic conflict far exceeding those shifting states of affections that might be found in free-style baroque recitatives or toccatas. Musicians of the new era valued contrast and development. They were eager to embrace character in action, character in motion. When Charles Rosen viewed the period of classical style, he explained:

> Dramatic expression, limited to the rendering of a sentiment or of a significant theatrical moment of crisis—in other words, to a dance movement full of individual character—had already found musical form in the High Baroque. But the later eighteenth century made further demands: the rendering of sentiment was not dramatic enough; Orestes must be shown going mad *without his being aware of it,* Fiordiligi must desire to yield while trying to resist, Cherubino fall in love without knowing what it is that he feels, and some years later, Florestan's despair give way and merge with his delirium and his apparently hopeless vision of Leonora.[22]

For Rosen, "dramatic sentiment was replaced by dramatic action."[23] After describing the movement "from joy through suspicion and outrage to final reconciliation" in the second-act finale of *Die Entführung aus dem Serail,* he continues:

[19]See the Prologue of Heartz, *Music in European Capitals,* 3-65, an exploration of "marked changes in culture and society" for a detailed account of visual and poetic enchantment.
[20]Louis-Emmanuel Jadin, "La Mort de Werther" printed in Frits Noske, *The Solo Song Outside German Speaking Countries* (Cologne: Arno Volk Verlag, 1958), 56-58.
[21]The villain in these plays and in the later grand opera was often the nobleman or some force in authority, the opposite of the Baroque representation of the nobility as heroic.
[22]Charles Rosen, *The Classical Style* (New York: Norton, 1971), 43.
[23]Rosen, *Classical Style,* 43.

The requirement of action applies equally well to non-operatic music: a minuet with a character of its own will no longer suffice. No two of J. S. Bach's minuets are alike in character, while there are a number of Haydn's that resemble each other almost to the point of confusion. Yet every one of Bach's has a seamless, almost uniform flow, which in Haydn becomes a series of articulated events—at times even surprising and shockingly dramatic events.[24]

Therefore we should extend our statement of the expressive ideal once again to read: *music of melodic orientation expressed in organized syntax of phrase and period linked to the expression of character often expressed in contrasting and developing ways as a kind of drama.* Character and drama could only be expressed in human terms. They are not ends in themselves but the means to make music communicative, possibly to allow music to move beyond entertainment or ritual values into a realm that makes the art capable of profound human feeling. Music might reach the consciousness of the human being, a condition that could truly be called promethean. Accessibility and humanity became linked in a way that furthered mankind's understanding of its own condition—the second gift of Prometheus. Goethe expressed it as he evoked the Titan forming men after his own image into "a race that will be like me, to suffer, to weep, to enjoy and be glad together," free of restraints of controlling gods.

The age can be divided historically into three fifty-year periods each beginning with a crucial event. The year 1750, marking the beginning of the Early Promethean Period, saw the publication of the prospectus of the *Encyclopédie* and the appearance the next year of the first volume of this epoch-making work, a challenge to long-accepted powers, the beginning of revolutionary thought. Within a few years of that date, the musical world saw the *guerre des bouffons,* crucial decisions in regard to opera, the publication of influential treatises by Geminiani, Marpurg, Emanuel Bach, Joachim Quantz, and Leopold Mozart, and the first appearance of the term "aesthetics."

The year 1800, marking the beginning of the Middle Promethean Period, saw the close of the revolutionary decade, the advent of the Napoleonic empire with its effects on western Europe, and the opening in 1799 of Pestalozzi's school at Bergdorf, an institution for the very young, a school that would have lasting effects on education. The musical world saw the enthusiastic welcome of Haydn's oratorio *The Creation* premiered in 1798, the culminating productions of rescue operas such as Cherubini's *Les deux journées* premiered in 1800 (and shortly Beethoven's *Fidelio*), and the utterly revolutionary work of the Eroica Symphony (1803-05)

The year 1850, marking the beginning of the Late Promethean Period, saw the establishment of order following the widespread revolutions of 1848-

---

[24]Rosen, *Classical Style,* 43.

49, the danger of death to musicians who supported the revolutions,[25] and the emigration of *Acht-und-Vierziger* to America. The musical world saw Liszt's retirement from the concert stage, his championing of Wagner and Berlioz, his composing of overtures that he would soon call *symphonic poems,* the publication of Wagner's major statements on the music drama, and the birth of the great quarrel about the New-German School.

The musician had become "master of his own thought" and was sending his works out to the new man who was also trying to be "master of his own thought," that second theme we have noted in the drama of Prometheus. It must be admitted, however, that a disjunction between technique and expression can be found in the works of those musical practitioners who exploited technique at the expense of profundity; those who cultivated trivial or purely virtuoso music.[26] Some had a strong technical gift, a flair for imitating, for "flash" that captured the public. In no way should this detract from the work of geniuses. Even in other eras, scholars and devotees have long recognized various levels of accomplishment. The term *Kleinmeister,* in current use in renaissance or baroque studies for those who used techniques without the communicative or imaginative ability of the most gifted creators, can also be applied to the Promethean Age.[27] These lesser musicians and their music need not become hindrances to adopting a new name anymore than the extravagance of the Baroque has interfered with the adoption of its name—although it once blinded thinkers to that generic term. We are now far enough removed from the Promethean Era's century and a half to interpret that span in terms of its ideals while still recognizing its problems and excesses. It is to the age's ideals, their development in vocal and instrumental music, and to actual musical examples that we now turn.

[25]Wagner mounted the barricades in Dresden. He just escaped capture in 1849 and lived in exile for many years. Alfred Julius Becher, composer and critic of Vienna, edited a revolutionary paper, *Der Radikale,* and for this activity was court-martialed and shot in 1848.

[26]The term *virtuoso* derives from the Indo-European root *viros* referring to "man." In its later usage as *virtuoso,* it denoted someone "skillful." For many years it meant a person of comprehensive musicianship. Thus when Bach was attacked by Scheibe, his defenders replied that he was a true *Virtuoso* not a mere *Musikant.* Today it can mean, according to *The American Heritage Dictionary* "a musician with masterly ability" but all too often it has been associated only with the secondary definition of "a brilliant performer." The Promethean Era has frequently been taxed with the most negative aspect of this word. On the positive side, the cultivation of virtuosity enlarged the horizons of musical performance and helped in the formation of the new music. Ralph P. Locke in "Paris: Centre of Intellectual Ferment," *The Early Romantic Era* (Englewood Cliffs, N.J.: Prentice Hall, 1991) 65, speaks of the piano virtuosos: "all of them contributed mightily towards the goal—about which Liszt, for one, was quite explicit—of gaining for instrumental music the kind of attention and respect that vocal music had long enjoyed and of establishing the piano as the central instrument of the Romantic age."

[27]The flood of music publishing in the Promethean Era included vast quantities of scores by *Kleinmeister.* Many journeymen never achieved mastership. The term "second fiddle" came to designate these musicians of lesser but often necessary ranks.

6. Vocal Art and the Expressive Ideal

The "cultivated" composers of this time adopted a type of music that emphasized melody. To be "natural" and therefore to be accessible to the new and more disparate audience, it would seem that music must forsake Baroque complexity and turn toward simple, easily understood melody. An example might be something like the setting of the following text.

N'est il Amour sous ton empire,	Cupid, do you have in your dominion
Que des rigueurs?	Only harshness?
S'il faut prevoir quand on souspire	Must one look forward when one sighs
Tous les malheurs,	To complete misfortune,
Tes biens n'offrent qu'un vain délire	Your comforts offer only a vain frenzy
Aux tenders coeurs.	To sensitive hearts.

N'est-il Amour sous ton empire
(Anon.) *Almanach des Muses*, 1765

This song tells, in ten stanzas, the tale of a young gentleman who has lost his lady love. The editors of the almanac frequently indicated their valuation of each song. In this case, they wrote that the poetry has "much simplicity, more feeling than intellect (*esprit*), that is the merit of this romance and what it should have."

Such simplicity in song had been apparent in French culture for a long period of time in the vaudevilles used in the fair theaters, tunes that were common property of the audience and the players. The new type, here illustrated, was freshly composed with text and melodies expressive of the interest in the gentle passions cultivated in the new era.

Jean-Jacques Rousseau favored simplicity above all else though not an uninspired style. Melody was to reign supreme; melody expressed in exact rhythm and meter fitted to the cadence of poetry. He approved bold modulations that could accord with sudden passionate expressions and hesitations. The accompaniments to this new melody should not be a jumble "heaping design upon design, instrument upon instrument."[1] No. The ensemble must:

> convey to the soul the sentiments which it is intended to arouse, all the parts must concur in reinforcing the impression of the subject; the harmony must serve only to make it more energetic, the accompaniment must embellish it without covering it up or disfiguring it; the bass, by a uniform and simple progression, must somehow guide the singer and the listener without either's perceiving it; in a word, the entire ensemble must at one time convey only one melody to the ear and only one idea to the mind.[2]

Rousseau thus championed a unity of poetry and music presented in the most "natural" fashion possible.[3]

In 1753, the same year as Rousseau's *Lettre*, the Berlin poet, translator of Batteux, and song collector, Carl Wilhelm Ramler, published a song collection, *Oden mit Melodien*. He collaborated with a lawyer-musician, Christian Gottfried Krause, who selected the melodies. The title "ode" given to these songs suggests something noble and exalted, having qualities of the ancient Greek odes but also some of the amiable, gentle, Anacreontic style of the German Enlightenment.[4] Ramler wrote the introduction to this collection.[5]

---

[1]Rousseau, *Lettre sur la musique française*; this quotation drawn from *Source Readings in Music History*, selected and annotated by Oliver Strunk (New York: Norton, 1950), 642.

[2]Rousseau, *Lettre*, Strunk *Source Readings*, 642-43. Rousseau continued, fifteen years after his *Lettre*, to oppose Baroque exaggeration in his *Dictionnaire de Musique* (1768). His ideas on music gained great currency not only from his *Dictionnaire* but from his musical articles in the *Encyclopédie*. Many writers, even into the nineteenth century, continued to quote him.

[3]See Appendix D.

[4]The collection opens with "An die Freude" of Hagedorn—"Joy, Goddess of my bright youth, Hear me! Let the songs that here resound satisfy your childen: What here rings forth, sounds through thee." The reprint edition of Ramler's *Lieder der Deutschen* (Stuttgart: J. B. Metzler, 1965) in an appendix by Alfred Anger gives the location of these poems in Ramler's *Oden mit Melodien* and his *Lyrische Bluhmenlese.*

[5]Ramler's introduction reads almost as something out of Rousseau, yet at this moment he could have known none of Rousseau's works with such a scene. Ramler's words suggest something like the grape harvest scene at M. de Wolmar's in *Julie ou la nouvelle Héloïse* in which commoner and estate wife alike join each other "singing and laughing the whole day long and the work goes (cont.)

The French have cultivated to a greater extent and more frequently the melodies of their songs and have made them in fact so *light and natural* that the whole country has become full of song and harmony. What a beautiful sight it is for an impartial citizen of the world and general friend of mankind when he sees among these people a farmer—with his grapes or with his onions in his hand—singing gaily and happily [italics inserted].[6]

Ramler would like to see this vision for the Germans as well.

We Germans study music everywhere yet in many large cities one hears nothing but opera arias. In these arias, however, song that is suitable for light pleasant singing—that can be taken up by every voice without trouble and even without accompaniment of another instrument—does not reign. If our vocal composers wrote without using the keyboard or thinking of it except for an added bass, then the taste for singing of our nation will become widespread. It should bring delight and social merriment everywhere.[7]

Composers soon began to aspire to something beyond this rustic simplicity. They sought character. At first the strophic song aroused one feeling, one general character, despite the changing nature of the poetic stanzas. Johann Philipp Kirnberger writing in Sulzer's *Allgemeine Theorie der schönen Künste* (1771) gave this advice:

Each composition, whether intended for songs with words or for instruments, must have a certain fixed character and must awaken in the mind of the listener feelings of a definite kind. How foolish it would be if the composer began his work without the character of his piece firmly decided.[8]

Even some ballads that told a complete story were, in the early stages of the era, set in a manner that repeated the same music for all stanzas. Composers, however, aware of the expressive possibilities in setting a changing poetic text, began to write modified strophic songs and still other songs that approached the through-composed Lied. Such compositions turned from the arousal of static character and moved toward drama and emotion, concepts and procedures that went far beyond Baroque ideals and embraced the outgoing, person-enhancing ideals of Prometheus, the Titan who would have man use his own capabilities, thoughts, and actions.

---

the better for it." In the evening they celebrate with song and dance before and after the communal supper. Rousseau's *Julie* was published in 1761, nine years later than Ramler's introduction. .

[6]Introduction to the *Oden mit Melodien* as printed in Max Friedlaender, *Das deutsche Lied im 18. Jahrhundert*, vol. 1, pt. 1 (Stuttgart: J. G. Cotta'sche Buchhandlung Nachfolger, 1902), 116.

[7]Friedlaender, *Deutsche Lied*, 116.

[8]Sulzer, "Ausdruck in der Musik," *Allgemeine Theorie der schönen Künste* (Leipzig, 1771), 111, as translated by Robert T. Laudon, "No One Can Possibly Mistake the Genre of this Composition," *Current Musicology* 25 (1978): 72. This article contains a brief summary of the various opinions concerning "character."

Gefammelte Werke
der Brüder
Chriſtian und Friedrich Leopold
Grafen zu Stolberg.

Fünfzehnter Band.

Hamburg 1823,
bei Perthes und Beſſer.

A vignette on the title page of a volume of works of the Counts zu Stolberg

This vignette, the frontispiece of Count Leopold's translation of Aeschylus's *Prometheus* depicts the Titan chained but striving to be free. To his left is his gift of fire, the eagle hovers over him, and the Oceanides gather at his feet.

Courtesy Wilson Library
Libraries of the University of Minnesota at Minneapolis

54

Sentiment and passion were essential to a promethean awakening of the individual. A person joined the new age not solely by the choice of reason but from a strong emotional attachment. Batteux, in his treatise establishing the fine arts, incorporated musical aspects when he spoke of lyric poetry:

Is it not song [*chant*] that gives life to joy, admiration, gratitude?...I do not see there any tableau, any painting. All is fire, feeling [*sentiment*], rapture.[9]

Music wanting to express "sentiments and passions"[10] joined poetry in a flexible unity.

And if these two parts [music and poetry] are inseparable one from the other, they ought to join together so that passions are subordinate to actions or actions to passions according to the means of expression that dominates the genre in which the artist is working.[11]

This union and its reaching out to the individual is apparent in a song such as *Süße heilige Natur* in Peter Schulz's *Lieder im Volkston* of 1785. The Graf zu Stolberg[12] conceived this poem as an entreaty to Nature—gentle as a child—"Sweet holy Nature let me go in your tracks, guide me with your hand as a child is led."[13]

The listener finds here a quiet character portrayed in music by slowly moving tempo and by soft tone. Schultz suggests the atmosphere he intends by marking the song *Sanft*, that is, gentle or tender. He begins each two-measure phrase of the melody with rest tones of the tonic E-flat major triad. The first, second, and fourth phrases return to this tonic harmony, an ultimate rest point. For the third phrase [*Leite mich*], he uses higher melodic notes and more active tones of the scale as he moves away from the persistent tonic chord—all designed to portray the "guiding" aspect of this line of the poem. He includes almost no dissonance save for the appoggiaturas at the cadence point of each phrase thereby confirming the *Sanft* character he assigned to the composition.

---

[9]Batteux, *Beaux Arts*, 244.

[10]Batteux, *Beaux Arts*, 270.

[11]Batteux, *Beaux Arts*, 270. His whole explanation is more complex than these excerpts can convey. He had to give an involved explanation because he was intent on using the theory of imitation as the one principle behind all the arts. Nonetheless, the excerpts give the essence of his immediate and strong reactions. There was at this time a vivid discussion of reason vs. passion. See Gay, *The Enlightenment,* 187-92, 281-87.

[12]The poet joined the Göttinger Hainbund shortly after its inception on September 12, 1772 when an alliance of poets found themselves in a grove [*Hain*] on a moonlit night and, inspired by nature and the emotional poetry of Klopstock, they pledged eternal friendship as they danced around an oak tree.

[13]Friedrich Leopold, Graf zu Stolberg, and his brother, Christian, were extremely sensitive to the new personal poetry and music.

Johann Abraham Peter Schulz, *Süße heilige Natur.*

A similar gentle and intimate appeal, a feeling new in the arts, can be found in a poetic lullaby, *Lied für Agnes, ihren Kleinen im Schlaf zu singen* whose words were written by the Count Leopold zu Stolberg. He indicated that this was to be sung to the Rousseau melody *Que le jour me dure* which was known as the "melody of three notes" using only the first three notes of the scale in various repetitive patterns—apt for the short lines of a lullaby.[14]

Schlafe, süßer Knabe,	Go to sleep, sweet boy,
Mir am Busen ein.	On my bosom,
Wohl mir, daß ich habe	Contented I am that I have
Dich, mein Bübelein	You, my little babe.

In the early days of Rousseau and Ramler, accompaniment still meant the traditional improvised one in which the accompanist realized his part guided by an unfigured or figured bass[15] It gradually took on a new meaning in the Promethean Age when composers began to write out fully annotated accompaniments designed specifically for a chosen text, for harmonic progression, for sensitivity to various parts of the singer's range, and for character and drama of that particular poetic-musical work.[16]

---

[14]Heartz, *European Capitals*, 21, cites Couperin's *Le Dodo* as an example of a restricted number of notes used for a lullaby.

[15]It was so defined in Rousseau's *Dictionnaire* and in Sulzer's *Allgemeine Theorie der schönen Künste.*

[16]The change from simple melody, to melody and bass part, to accompanied melody can be seen in the music examples that Max Friedlaender presents in chronological order in *Das deutsche Lied im 18. Jahrhundert* vol. 1, pt. 2. Rousseau wrote some notated accompaniments in relatively simple style. Jean-Benjamin de La Borde published four volumes of *Choix de chansons mises en musique* (1772-75), all chansons with fully notated accompaniments. This "new" style of accompaniment coincides with the emergence of the piano, an instrument ideally suited to a supporting (cont.)

Schubert's setting (D. 774) of Friedrich Leopold zu Stolberg's barcarolle,[17] *Auf dem Wasser zu singen,* can illustrate the way that an accompaniment, a shift of tonality, and various melodic devices can create a sense of character quite beyond the simple one that Schultz had evoked. The poem expresses two themes: (1) the changing lights of sunset glinting upon the water and (2) the comparison of the voyage of a boat to the voyage of the soul as it arrives in the fullness of time. The poet announces this crux of the poem in the third and fourth lines of the first stanza: "Ah, upon the joyful soft-gleaming waves, glides the soul like the boat" and at similar lines in the last two stanzas.

Mitten im Schimmer der spiegelnden Wellen

Gleitet, wie Schwäne, der wankende Kahn;

Ach, auf der Freude sanft-schimmenden Wellen

Gleitet die Seele dahin wie der Kahn.

Denn von dem Himmel herab auf die Wellen

Tanzet das Abendroth rund um den Kahn.

At twilight in mirroring waves

Swanlike, the wavering boat glides;

Ah, upon the joyful soft-gleaming waves,

The soul like the boat glides.

Then from the heavens, down upon the waves

The sunset dances round about the boat.

The translation above is simply for the basic meaning; no attempt has been made to mimic the style. The poem is both naïve and impressionistic at the same time. The third word is indeed "shimmer" but in dialect is "twilight." A number of sounds are repeated frequently in exact consonant or nearly exact vowel sounds—Schimmer, spiegelnden, Schwäne—wankende, Kahn, Ach, sanft, dahin, herab, tanzet, Abendroth. Somewhat as a masterstroke—or perhaps a stunt— Leopold zu Stolberg constructed each of his three stanzas with perfect

---

or interpretive role. It should be noted immediately that there also grew up a repertory of stereotype accompaniment figures—often parodied as ump-pah sounds—much used by those who wanted quick success in the commercial market. Even these clichés could be bent to the new style by dynamic shading to suit soft or climatic passages, possibilities for the piano or for the guitar or harp.

[17]The numerous styles of barcarolle are discussed by Rodney Stenning Edgecombe, "On the limits of Genre: Some Nineteenth-Century Barcaroles," *19th Century Music* 34 (2001): 252-67. Carl Dahlhaus discussed the difficulties of determining the limits of various genres at this time in "Zur Problematik der musikalischen Gattungen im 19. Jahrundert," *Gattungen der Musik in Einzeldarstellungen: Gedenkschrift für Leo Schrade,* vol. 1 (Bern: Franke, 1973), 840-95.

Franz Schubert, *Auf dem Waser zu singen.*

symmetry. Even the "glittering" words and the word "heaven" appear at identical metric points within the three stanzas. The final lines project a deeper meaning of the poem, a movement from the material world to the infinite—Stanza One "dances the sunset around about the boat;" Stanza Two, "breathes the soul in ever growing rosy light;" and Stanza Three "the soul itself vanishes in the passage of time." Whatever may be our contemporary judgment, the poem was extremely popular at the time.

Schubert, keenly aware of the poetic character, the persistent reference to shimmering light reflected on the waves, wrote an piano accompaniment consisting of a steady rhythm of descending sixteenth notes with pulsing 2-note slurs to suggest glinting, subtly shifting light (the introduction is omitted in the musical example). So important is this musical figure to his concept of the poem that he incorporated it into the vocal line itself (ms. 2, 4-6, and 9-10) although he used traditional dotted rhythms of the barcarolle for the vocal melody as well, thereby matching the dactyls of the poetry, and representing the pulsing of the boat (ms. 1, 3, 7, 11, 14-17, and 20).

To mark the change of emphasis as the poet compares the movement of the boat to the gliding of the soul (lines 3 and 4), Schubert shifts to the mediant-major (ms. 5-7) by harmonizing the C-flat of the tonic chord as root of a major triad in order to give a whole new color to the crux of the poem. Then in order to suggest the mystery of the heavens from whence light comes, he prolongs an equivocal diminished-seventh chord (ms. 13-15).

To depict the words "heaven" and "heights" Schubert placed these words on the highest notes of the vocal melody, a vivid musical device, the rhetorical figure of hypotyposis. Finally to call attention to the conclusion of each stanza, he introduced a high sustained note (ms. 18-19).

Schubert employs the minor mode—suggesting the intrinsic sorrow of man's passing time on earth—and maintained this with the one expressive exception noted above (ms. 5-11) until the conclusion of each stanza (m. 19) at which point the piano carries the listener into the major mode confirming that the journey has been both shining and ultimately worthwhile.

Within this short Lied—which unfolds naturally and with a folk-like simplicity matching the naiveté of the poem—Schubert created a state of heightened character with a fuller union of word and tone than Batteux could have imagined. It shows us how composers of the age were enlarging their concept of the expressive ideal beyond that of "simplicity" to "heightened character," and even to "incipient drama."

With ingenious accompaniments, less dependence on rhetoric alone in building a melodic line, and great sensitivity to literary texts, composers were erecting an amazing art that reached the divine heights associated with the very name of poetry. In its embrace of topics of personal life, the art reached out to the rapidly burgeoning public showing them the profundity of a new musical-poetic art[18]—achieved through the technological marvel of the piano and composers' mastery "of their own thought," the two-pronged gift of Prometheus to mankind. In the process, the Middle Promethean Period (1800-1850), the time of this Schubert song, realized more fully what was already present in embryo during the Early Period (1750-1800).

The newly developed style became widely accepted. It meets the test of a truly promethean manner that must go out to a large public. Songs were printed in quantities that seem almost incredible. Max Friedlaender lists 762 *Liedersammlungen* between the years 1750 and 1799.[19]

Strands of poetry and music joined hands in the almanacs of the eighteenth century. Simple songs in this format began to be published in 1765 by the newly-founded Parisian *Almanach des Muses* that became the model for later almanacs. This popular yearly publication usually included three or four chansons in each issue, the poetry in the body of the text and the engraved melodies grouped together near the end of the volume just before the notices on the poetic publications and theatrical performances of the year.[20] The songs displayed the principles put forth by Rousseau: simple melodies in symmetrical units with

---

[18]Schubert's Lieder only slowly became known and appreciated through a few transcendent performances and especially through the Liszt transcriptions that introduced the larger public to them. Just as literacy was growing slowly, so was the ability of audiences to understand the new music.

[19]Friedlaender, *Deutsche Lied*, 6-62 (Bibliography).

[20]The series under the impetus of Sautreau de Marsy and published by Delalain, eventually reached 65 volumes. It was widely imitated. Frédéric Lachèvre has published a *Bibliographie sommaire de l'Almanach des Muses* (Paris: L. Giraud Badin, 1928). Music was included steadily for 16 years when suddenly the almanac switched to poetry alone and welcomed many complex poetical works unsuitable for music.

The simple setting of *Auf dem Wasser zu singen* in a book of convivial activities

Der angenehme Gesellschafter: eine Sammlung ganz neuer Unterhaltungs, Scherz-pfander-Kasten-Wurfel-und anderer Spiele, Karten-Rechnen und verschiedener mechanischer und anderer Taschenspielerkunststücke, Andekdoten, Räthseln &c. dann trink-und anderer Lieder mit dazu gestochener Musik, third edition (Gatz: J. A. Kienrich, 1794). Note that the volume has been well used with the wear and tear during two centuries showing.

Courtesy Special Collections and Rare Books
Libraries of the University of Minnesota at Minneapolis

very little ornament.[21] They were presented as melody alone, or melody with a bass part, and rarely with a written accompaniment.[22]

Heinrich Christian Boie and Friedrich Wilhelm Gotter, aware of the success of the *Almanach des Muses*, put out in 1770 an *Almanach der deutschen Musen*, the first in a long series widely known in German-speaking lands. It had contents similar to its French model: lyric poems selected from the poetry of the year plus interspersed songs. Like the French model, this *Musenalmanach* inspired a

---

[21]Except for an occasional trill on the penultimate note at the cadence.
[22]As, for instance, the Romance by M. de Leyre "Je l'ai planté" to which Rousseau supplied a melody with a simple written-out accompaniment of broken chord patterns.

host of imitations under the auspices of various editors and organizations.[23] A number of Mozart songs were published in the *Wienerischer Musenalmanach* and Beethoven and Schubert songs appeared in such almanacs and other diverse publications.[24]

Even in the books devoted to games, riddles, and anecdotes suitable for convivial gatherings, songs—which Ramler had promised could "bring delight and social merriment everywhere"—formed one section. *Der angenehme Gesellschafter* of 1794, for instance, included a section of Lieder: words within the publication and their simple unornamented melodies without bass parts or accompaniments placed in a foldout section at the end of the volume. [25]

We have arrived at the Age of Song, the Age of Melody. Music has become accessible, the promethean "fire going out to all mankind." It went to singers who reveled in the joy of performance. It reached people at many levels of society. It entertained theatergoers not only in *opéras comiques* and in *Singspiele* but also in *folies, comédies mêlée d'ariettes*, and other plays with interpolated songs. As the years went by, more and more music lovers, through increased education, found themselves able to appreciate more complex developments as the vocal composers moved in later years from Romance to the Mélodie, from simple Lieder to the Kunstlied or the Liederzyklus. and from aria to scena.

[23]Margaret Mahony Stoljar, in *Poetry and Song in Late Eighteenth Century Germany, A Study in the Musical Sturm und Drang* (London: Croom Helm, 1985), presents in her first chapter a survey in English—with reference to the German sources—of still more of the varied ways in which poetry and song reached out to society of the day.

[24]See Ewan West, "The Musenalmanach and Viennese Song, 1770-1830," *Music and Letters* 67/1 (January 1986): 37-49. Our tidy editions sometimes give a wrong impression of the original format of songs and novels.

[25]Such books are somewhat rare in collections. It appears however that more investigation might prove fruitful in tracing the acceptance of song among new auditors. Taschenbücher and almanacs reveal much about the dissemination of new ideas and might have relevance for music as well. For England, there is a remarkable essay, "Popular entertainment and instruction, literary and dramatic: chapbooks, advice books, almanacs, ballads, farces, pantomimes, prints and shows" by Lance Bertelsen published in *The Cambridge History of English Literature, 1660-1780*, ed. John Richetti (Cambridge: Cambridge University Press, 2005), 61-86.

7. Instrumental Art and the Expressive Ideal

In the beginning years of the era, three gifted German instrumentalists put forth their ideas on their favored instruments and the new style. Johann Joachim Quantz published a *Versuch einer Anweisung die Flöte traversière zu spielen* (1752), Emanuel Bach, a *Versuch über die wahre Art, das Clavier zu spielen* (1753), and Leopold Mozart, a *Versuch einer gründlichen Violinschule* (1756). All became landmarks in musical education, an essential part of the promethean reaching out to the newly involved public. Quantz's and Mozart's essays were soon translated and used widely.[1] Emanuel Bach's essay was revised and republished several times together with a remarkable number of related compositions serving as guideposts for the pupil.[2]

Of the three, Quantz devoted the most space to explanations of the older and newer musical styles. The older he called "elaborate," the newer, "gallant."[3] He did not champion one or the other but was more concerned with how to perform, understand, and judge each.

In regard to melody, that crucial element in the new style, he believed that a solo part in a concerto "must be in part singing, while the ingratiating should be in part relieved by brilliant, melodious, harmonious passages, always suited to the instrument"[4] and that, for the Adagio, "composers have for some time past begun to make their Adagios more singing…the melody must be just as touching and expressive as though there were words below it."[5]

---

[1] Quantz's essay was issued simultaneously in French, then in Dutch (1754), Italian (1779), and partially in English (1780). Leopold Mozart's method was reissued and enlarged several times and appeared in Dutch (1766) and French (1770). The transverse flute, Quantz's instrument, which was now replacing the Baroque recorder, deserves a social history similar to that of Loesser's for the piano. A start in this direction is David Eagle, "A Constant Passion and a Constant Pursuit, A Social History of Flute-playing in England from 1800 to 1851" (Ph.D. diss. University of Minnesota, 1977).

[2] Emanuel Bach's *Essay* was undoubtedly the most practical compendium, particularly when used in conjunction with the *Probestücke*, and companion sonatas. The *Essay* continued to be printed and revised through 1797 and was used far beyond that date.

[3] Strunk, *Source Readings*, 583. Quantz made this distinction in regard to the Trio and a similar one in differentiating the Concerto Grosso with many players from the Concerto da Camera for a soloist.

[4] Strunk, *Source Readings*, 584. This is found in his description of the concerto but he later tells us that, with these principles, one may proceed to the other genres

[5] Strunk, *Source Readings*, 586-87.

Instrumental music of the Early Promethean Period (1750-1800) did indeed, as Quantz perceived, have certain "singing" features. That quality that Quantz noticed has today become known as the "singing allegro." It brings the tuneful melodic line into prominence by subordinating the accompaniment and by a slow harmonic rhythm that allows time for the melody to expand. Keyboard composers frequently used only a melody and a bass, or sometimes, a melody and a stereotyped accompaniment such as the Alberti bass or the murky. The result was *simple* instrumental music that went out to delighted amateurs— although we should hasten to add that many gifted composers wrote sonatas in a more complex manner.[6]

The instrumental composers of the era also adopted a division into equal phrase and period lengths similar to that of song and dance music. Periodicity helped the listener to grasp the structure, concentrate attention on the melody, and assist in remembering the tune. Just as an established syntax in language enables the speaker or writer to be easily understood, so an established standard of utterance in musical language helped the auditor to grasp the musical thought and to find points of emphasis as the composer obeyed or varied that syntax— a practice supporting the promethean ideal of accessibility for those willing to accept the new instrumental idiom.[7]

This sort of music could have been directly based on dance music or folk-like song. Haydn did so at times. However, there does not seem to have been a widespread movement to incorporate known songs and dances into instrumental compositions; instead, composers absorbed some of the current musical idioms and made them their own. William Newman discussed the possibility of imitating dance or song and concluded:

> It is both more applicable and more accurate to think of the composer as adapting to his artistic uses certain characteristic melodic elements, scale types, and phrase-and-period structures that had become common property.[8]

---

[6]See Appendix E.

[7]Rousseau, and others who believed vocal music to be the crown of the art found the new instrumental style confusing. Some of his attitude may have stemmed from sonatas that were more hand exercises than character pieces. The attitude of these early detractors of the new style is summed up in the bon mot attributed to Fontenelle: *Sonate, que me veux tu?*

[8]Newman, *Sonata in the Classic Era*, 125-26. At times, when dances were incorporated into one of the imposing genres such as the symphony, they aroused downright opposition in conservative circles as Haydn's Symphony Number 28 did in Leipzig.

> [This] Symphony has been put into a bearable form not long ago by one of our [Leipzig] composers and the excrescences [Auswüchse] removed; the last movement in six-eight time has been left out of the print altogether; it would been better to have omitted the silly trio, together with the minuet.

(H. C. Robbins Landon, *The Symphonies of Joseph Haydn* [London: Universal Edition, 1955], 264) quoting J. A. Hiller in the *Wöchenliche Nachrichten und Anmerkungen, die Musik betreffend, auf das Jahr 1770.*

By the end of the eighteenth century and beginning of the nineteenth, melody expressed in balanced phrases and periods had become so customary that that common practice entered theoretical literature. Two of the most important treatises, Christoph Koch's *Versuch einer Anleitung zur Composition* (3 volumes, 1782-1793) and Anton Reicha's *Traité de Mélodie* (1814), outlined the structure of the "period" and its smaller and larger units which, when organized into the complete structure of a movement, created the particular "form" of the composition, a "form" described through its melodic and tonal structure. Above all, this culminated in the sonata form or sonata principle that formed a wonderfully flexible spine for so much promethean music.

Like their vocal counterparts, instrumental works were greeted with acclaim not simply because of regularity of syntax and form but also because of the character that was conveyed by their melodies. Composers began to give the performer detailed directions for the interpretation of melodic units—tempo, articulation,[9] degrees of loudness and softness—things seldom indicated in the Baroque Age but which grew ever more important in the new era. By the middle and late periods, composers titled works to suggest general moods: nocturnes, fantasies, ballades, scherzos. Composers wanted coherent musical shapes and wished to make these shapes *simultaneously* expressive to the auditor.[10]

The instrumental equivalent of literary "Characters" is the *Characterstück*, the Character Piece, written for keyboard instruments. Toward the end of the Baroque Era, François Couperin sought in his *Pièces de clavecin, premier livre* (1713) an individuality that he indicated by exact titles.

> I have always had an object in mind when composing all these pieces, suggested to me by various events or circumstances. Thus the titles relate to ideas that have occurred to me, and I shall be forgiven if I do not account for them. However, since among these titles there are several which seem to flatter me, I should point out that the pieces in question are in a sense portraits, which, under my fingers, have been found on occasion to be remarkable likenesses. Most of these flattering

[9]Early keyboard sonatas used only a limited amount of articulation, frequently only slash strokes for staccato. Haydn provided models of detailed articulation in his string quartets, where his involved articulation coupled with an exploitation of the registers of the instruments provides a type of orchestral interplay within the confines of the quartet.

[10]Frequently the auditor only became aware of the feeling in contemplation after the fact or perhaps in a sudden momentary recognition during the performance. Today we are beginning to have detailed information on the brain and know that all of our senses communicate through the brain stem and other lower centers of the brain, centers that give emotional quality, before being referred to the centers of consciousness and rationality. This understanding has given rise to the expression that "man is a feeling animal that thinks." This complicated subject, still in its formative stages, cannot be undertaken here. The reader is referred to the works of Gerald M. Edelman and others and especially to Antonio Damasio, *The Feeling of What Happens, Body and Emotion in the Making of Consciousness* (New York: Harcourt, 1999). My essay "The Elements of Expression in Music: A Psychological Viewpoint" is scheduled to appear in *The International Review of the Aesthetics and Sociology of Music* 37/2 (Dec. 2006).

titles are given rather to the amiable originals which I have sought to portray, than to the settings which I have drawn from them.[11]

In the new era, this type of piece appeared in collections by individual composers under the generic title of *Handstücke* or *Klavierstücke*.[12] They also were published frequently in anthologies by various composers—sometimes with interspersed songs. These periodical miscellanies[13] were more or less the instrumental equivalents of musical-poetic almanacs.

Individual pieces were given evocative titles. Daniel Gottlob Türk suggested the mood of the composition by such headings as *Eye popeya!* (Hushabye, Baby) or *Hans ohne Sorgen* (Carefree Hans).[14] One could easily assume that Türk's titles were given simply to be agreeable, intriguing, and edifying for young children. Türk, however, intended even in his tiny pieces to establish character. He carefully marked each piece with tempo and dynamic indications, and, though he maintained that these simple pieces ought to depict a person or a feeling, yet he believed that "*all* compositions should have a character "[my italics].[15] Just a few years before Türk, Christian Gottlob Neefe, Beethoven's teacher, had written in a similar vein, "The great and true artist paints and says nothing of it, the bungler tells us all and paints nothing."[16]

The character of *Sorgenlose Heiterkeit* (Carefree mirth), for instance, is conveyed by major mode, lively tempo, upbeat entry, contrast of piano and forte phrases, and no strain of dissonance.

---

[11]*Pièces de clavecin, premier livre*, ed. Kenneth Gilbert (Paris: Heugel, 1972), xxii. Precise portrayal is even more marked in Couperin's later books (1716-17, 1722, and 1730). Such self-effacing modesty as Couperin displays is one of the qualities prized by the *honnête homme*. It should be noted that Couperin exceeded the stricter aspects of the doctrine of the affections by reference to living contemporaries, by using registers of bass or treble for complete pieces, and by the consistent use of several contrast sections to vie with his main character's expressive musical theme. Couperin was already on the road to the new style even as Sebastian Bach was in some late compositions.

[12]The *Handstücke* sometimes leaned more toward hand exercises without distinctive character as, for instance, the *Blumenlese* and *Neue Blumenlese* in which very early compositions of Beethoven were printed.

[13]Often these miscellanies lasted but a short time but as one folded, another came into contention.

[14]In Türk's *Handstücke für angehende Klavierspieler* (1792, 1795). Willy Kahl, in the series *Anthology of Music*, includes two of these compositions in his collection, *The Character Piece* (Cologne: Arno Volk Verlag, 1961), 43-44. It should be pointed out that the purpose of Türk's book is educational and that the majority of the pieces carry purely musical titles such as *Die Tonleiter, Der Pralltriller, Die Bindung*, etc. Nonetheless even these are composed with an appropriate character in mind. There seems to be a tendency for scholars to place teaching literature beyond serious consideration. While that literature is, of course, not of the profundity of greater art works, it served an important purpose in this age. It does seem time to acknowledge the contributions that made musical literacy and love of the art widely available. The role of women is particularly noteworthy. Nearly all of the "great masters" spent untold hours with students. Even Hugo Riemann taught classes of young children and instructed his students in pedagogy.

[15]Daniel Gottlob Türk, *Klavierschule* (Leipzig and Halle, 1789), 395.

[16]Christian Gottlob Neefe, *Dilettanterien* (Bonn, 1785), 133.

Daniel Gottlob Türk, *Sorgenlose Heiterkeit.*

Musical character could be established by the intrinsic qualities of melodic motion and tension made even more expressive by imaginative accompaniments and appropriate harmony, the whole supplemented by directions for the performer's interpretation. As the art moved from its early days to the Middle and Late Promethean Periods, words such as espressivo, più mosso, crescendo, diminuendo, and a host of poetic words—piangendo, mesto, giocoso, leggiero, and so on—began to pepper the scores in order to help the performer make character ever more precise.

When the Prometheans moved beyond the simple portrayal of *one* character and began to use *multiple* musical ideas within a single movement, a radical change took place marking a distinct break with ideals of the past. A keyword became *emotion*, an old word with a new urgency.[17] The feeling quality of a melody could be enhanced, developed, or changed in manifold ways—if it appeared in the timbre of a particular instrument, with various harmonies or counterpoints, following an introduction, after an energetic non-thematic transition, by modulation to a new tonality, after punctuation points and in other imaginative ways. When a melody, now raised to the level of a *theme*, was placed thus in contrast or competition with other elements, the net result went beyond simple "character" and became the conveyer of complex "emotion."

[17]The term "emotion"—in English, French, and German—has a long history stemming from its basic concept: that of motion. In the mid-eighteenth century, some artists began to give it a prominent place—in the Storm and Stress Movement for instance. As the age became more heated, so emotion became ever more an essential in art. Alphonse de Lamartine explained the situation in his later preface (1849) to his *Méditations poétiques* (1820): "I am the first that made poetry descend from Parnassus and who has given to what is called the muse, in place of the seven strings of convention, the very fibers of man's heart, touched and moved by innumerable stirrings of the soul and of nature."

A striking example of this new approach can be found in the Andante of Mozart's Piano Concerto in E-flat Major, K 482 (1785). The preceding Allegro concludes with ten powerful measures of repeated cadential patterns and a final four measures on a reiterated E-flat Major chord. The Andante begins in C Minor.

Wolfgang Amadeus Mozart, The Andante theme of the Concerto in E-flat Major, K. 482.

The muted first violins accompanied only by muted strings announce a theme. The dark sounds of the G and D strings and a dissonant appoggiatura motive characterize the first period (12 bars, cadence in E-flat Major). Sequences of low and high notes—moving upward—intensify the middle period (8 bars, cadence in G Minor) with an arrival point that avoids the bright sound of the major dominant chord. The opening idea returns in C Minor rising to an intense and unexpected D-flat in the final period (12 bars, cadence in C Minor). At no time does Mozart use the brilliant E string.

In addition to the tensions of the appoggiaturas and the somber timbre, the motion in triple meter has no touch of forward march-like character. It revolves and falls back upon itself. The most pointed gesture of the theme, "motive a," a prolonged appoggiatura, builds through repetition (mm. 5-7) toward a point of great strain on a ninth chord marked sforzato-piano (m. 8). The built-up tension can only be released by a short dramatic silence on the strong beat just before the cadence almost as if one were submitting to a force. In the concluding period, "motive a" is resumed, then repeated on a higher D-flat (mm. 23-24) before yet another statement of the appoggiatura (mm. 25-26). At last we reach the tense repeated supertonic seventh, again marked sforzato-piano, before a point of silence and the cadence in C Minor. It is as if a person is mourning a great loss and finding it nearly impossible to recover.[18]

Within the total movement, this theme is modified three times: first, by a simple variation for the piano (pitched an octave above the string presentation), second, by a forte outburst of the theme accompanied by turbulent thirty-second notes in the bass register of the piano, a sort of protest:

and finally, by the alternation of full-orchestra dramatic statements and soft answers of the piano on succeeding phrases of the theme. Eventually the orchestra is quieted. A coda hints at an ending in major mode that, however, never succeeds. The movement trails off quietly in minor.

The feeling quality of the theme, established by its intrinsic motion and tension, is further heightened through contrast with two intervening episodes scored for winds and placed between variations 2 and 3, then between 3 and 4: the first episode in E-flat Major,

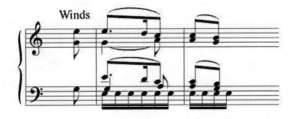

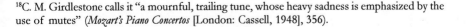

[18]C. M. Girdlestone calls it "a mournful, trailing tune, whose heavy sadness is emphasized by the use of mutes" (*Mozart's Piano Concertos* [London: Cassell, 1948], 356).

a steadily moving confirmation in the winds of the major mode, and a second episode in C Major, of almost pastoral nature established by a dialogue between flute and bassoon.

The Andante is a grieving statement with tensions and dramatic pauses, relieved by interludes, followed in the middle of the movement by violent protest—must it be—until finally the protagonist at the piano, following perhaps the gentle flute of the second interlude, calms the orchestral force and submits to the inevitable.

The interest that composers and audiences took in the slow movement marks yet one more significant change in style and stylistic expectation. The slow movement in the sinfonia had been the shortest and least developed of the traditional three movements. Even in the concerto it frequently continued, at first, the baroque tradition of a movement marked by an ostinato figure or a perfunctory transition between the *important* fast movements. Now, during the Early Promethean Period, this movement became a fully conceived composition that could become the expressive focal point of the complete work, an expressive foil for the traditionally brilliant outer movements. This was evident in Haydn's work from the 1770s on. According to story, Haydn even requested the slow movement of his *Trauersinfonie* to be played at his funeral. A number of his slow movements used muted strings. When confronted with the commission to write music for the Service of the Seven Last Words at Cadiz, he recognized the challenge of writing seven slow movements worthy of the convictions he shared.

Mozart, too, raised the slow movement to a new pinnacle. We have evidence from a letter of Mozart's father, Leopold, of the effect that the Andante of the Concerto in E-Flat Major had upon its first audience. Towards the end of 1785, Mozart himself was so busy with the composition of *Le Nozze di Figaro* and with his students that he scarcely had time to write.[19] Nonetheless, he managed one letter to his father who relayed the news on to his daughter, Nannerl.

> Meanwhile to two letters of mine I have had only one reply from your brother, dated December 28th, in which he said that he gave without much preparation three subscription concerts for 120 subscribers, that he composed for this purpose

[19]Leopold to his daughter, Salzburg, 11 November 1785, *The Letters of Mozart and His Family*, ed. and trans. Emily Anderson, 2nd ed. (New York: St. Martin's, 1966), 893.

a new piano concerto in E-flat, in which (a rather unusual occurrence!) he had had to repeat the Andante.[20]

This example of the profound expressive nature of what could be drawn from the melodically-oriented style shows a promethean grasp of new powers, a use of human talent the Titan envisioned for mankind. He gave humanity the fundamentals upon which they could build—words, numbers, and other basics—but all designed to release his earthly people from the bondage of ignorance. He did not give them static rules that they were forced to obey. So in the era of 1750-1900, artists found a new world opened to them. It started with a simpler style superceding the baroque style and progressed through the artists' sensitivity—to a world of expressive, dramatically-oriented promethean freedom.

If instrumental compositions of the era were to exemplify the promethean ideal of going out to all mankind, then it is evident from the foregoing that they had to reach a variety of audiences, professional and amateur, and to reach them in significant numbers. Sonatas and symphonies, often produced in sets of six or twelve in one publication—following the late baroque tradition found in works by Corelli, Händel, or Vivaldi—testify in their mass production to their popularity. They went out both to major centers and outposts of Europe. Not only did the prospective performer receive groups of musical pieces, but he or she could even subscribe to monthly or yearly sets—*Monatschriften, Periodical Overtures, Journals,* and *Collections*—designed to entice the eager keyboardist or group of chamber players.[21] (Illustration next page.)

No one instrumental series ran for a long uninterrupted series as the almanacs did for song literature. Still new publications sprang up frequently so that the seeker was always provided with scores at the music dealer or the lending library.

The sonata literature encompassed a vast audience comparable to the audience for the song literature written in the new accessible style. William Newman found 3,200 separate sonatas to study in the period from 1750 through 1828, but he estimated that there existed five times that many.[22] In the professional category, Jan LaRue was able to list over 13,000 separate works in his monumental catalogue of symphonies of the time span from *c.* 1720 to *c.* 1810. Year by year, the number of public concerts grew from the garden concerts to the more formal ones. Some of these were even dignified by a new term, philharmonic, a glorious name fraught with significance for the ever-widening audience.

---

[20]Leopold to his daughter, Salzburg, 12 November 1785, *Letters,* 895.
[21]Examples abound in François Lesure, *Recueils imprimés du XVIIIe Siècle,* RISM series, B/2.
[22]Newman, *Sonata in the Classic Era,* Chap. 4, The Spread of the Classic Sonata, 59-79.

Cover page of Jomelli's *Periodical Overture in 8 Parts, Number xiiii.*

Note that the publication was a practical one of parts for the individual players who waited for the latest monthly symphony. Score publication was rare particularly in the Early to Middle Promethean Periods. Note also that the cover plate is a passepartout cover made so that various composer's names could be inserted. In a slightly earlier edition of this work by Preston and Son, Jomelli's insert was even a bit askew. Overture was a frequent name for symphony in England.

Courtesy of The Newberry Library

72

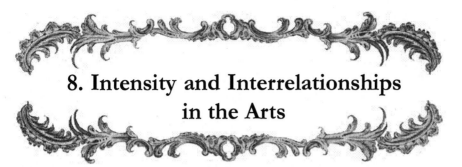

8. Intensity and Interrelationships in the Arts

After the initial steps in the eighteenth century, music and the other arts grew more ardent and extreme in attempting to capture the listener's, reader's, and viewer's feelings as aroused by the artwork itself. Drama became a major goal. Furthermore, musicians and allied artists believed they could gain ever greater emotional expression through a combination of the arts.[1] The arts had been invested with a new dignity; they had become from mid-eighteenth century the *beaux arts*, fine arts entitled to a special place in life. No longer did one identify a practitioner solely as painter, musician, writer, poet, sculptor, or dancer, but as an *artist*, a person concerned with the flourishing of *all* the arts.

Performance arts, opera and drama,[2] called upon the panoply to make a hybrid type in which the various arts were combined in the service of dramatic force,[3] that essential of the new style. So also with ballet. Formalities of the Baroque Era began to disappear in the art of dance. Marie Sallé dared before 1740 to substitute a thin muslin costume for the heavy court dress that had been considered obligatory. Dancers' masks began to disappear. Courtly, entertaining, and diverting theater dance seemed out of date. Pantomime and action became essentials of the *ballet d'action,* as it moved toward goals of character and emotion.

Few persons had as much ability and as much opportunity to learn the various arts and combine them into a new unity as the dancer/choreographer,

[1]Marsha L. Morton and Peter L. Schmunk, editors, *The Arts Entwined* (New York: Garland, 2000), a collection of essays, contains much bibliographic information. Morton's introductory essay, "From the Other Side," presents a thoughtful consideration of issues and methods.

[2]Opera became "grand opera" in the nineteenth century, an "elevated" term that increased its attraction but also one that signified a union of the arts. William Crosten, *French Grand Opera, An Art and a Business* (New York: Kings Crown, 1948), 3, remarked after his study of the style, "It can hardly be overemphasized that French opera of the 1830s displays a real union, not a senseless mélange of arts."

[3]A number of thinkers proposed a series of steps in culture culminating in drama, that essential of the modern style. One of the most telling statements was made by Victor Hugo in the preface to his verse play, *Cromwell* (1827): "Poetry has three ages, each corresponding to an epoch in society: the ode, the epic, the drama. Primitive times are lyric, ancient times are epic, modern times are dramatic. The ode sings of eternity, the epic makes history solemn, the drama paints life...There are the three faces of youth, virility, and age...Society begins indeed by singing of what it dreams, then tells of what it accomplishes, and finally begins to paint what it thinks. It is, let us say in passing, for this last reason that drama, uniting the most opposite qualities, can be at the same time full of profundity and full of enhancement, philosophical and picturesque."

Salvatore Viganò (1769-1821). He received a thorough training in movement and dance from his father and from his family. He married Maria Medina, a remarkable ballerina. Together they rose to the top rank of performers. In 1789, he became initiated into the world of pantomime as a student of the *ballet d'action* master, Jean Berger Dauberval. Viganò studied music with his uncle, Luigi Boccherini, and progressed to the point of composing a small opera buffa. Viganò rounded off his amazing studies with painting, thereby becoming a master with the full panoply of the arts at his command.

Viganò mounted a coreodrama[4] of *Prometheus* twice: once in Vienna (1801) with music by Beethoven, and a second time in Milan (1813) with music by Beethoven, Haydn, Mozart, Weigl, and others.[5] The first production, a two act ballet, *Gli uomini di Prometeo,* or *Die Geschöpfe des Prometheus,* The Creatures [or Creations] of Prometheus,[6] portrays how the two arts of music and dance could bring human feeling and human conscience to the raw clay figures of a woman and a man, figures that Prometheus had endowed with life. This ballet is therefore often referred to by its subtitle, *The Power of Music and Dance.*[7]

The gifted choreographer realized after the first producion that there was more profundity to the theme than he had been able to realize. Not until his appointment to the Milanese Court Theater of La Scala in the season of 1811-12 was he able to change his dreams into reality.[8] In the spring of 1813, during his second season, Viganò scored his first great triumph at Milan with *Prometeo,* a dance-drama in six acts, given before an audience of 3,000 astounded people. It began in the great vortex of chaos when the sun and spheres were born. Clustered on a mountain, as light appears, are Prometheus, the Virtues, the Arts, and Muses. Humans led by a pair—Eone, the woman, and Lino, the man[9]— are gradually instructed and brought out of their wild state. The story unfolds in great detail until the final release of Prometheus by Heracles and followed by the Titan's reconciliation with Zeus.[10]

---

[4]This term was used by Viganò's biographer, Carlo Ritorni, *Commentarii della Vita e delle Opere Coreodrammatiche di Salvatore Viganò e della coregrafia e de' corepei* (Milan, 1838*).*

[5]"Mayland, den 29sten May," *Allgemeine musikalische Zeitschrift* (June 1813): 434-436.

[6]The title seemed at the time—and in later judgment—to be treading upon the popularity of Haydn's *Die Schöpfung* (April of 1798 and numerous performances thereafter). See H. C. Robbins Landon, *Haydn, Chronicle and Works,* 5 vols. (Bloomington: Indiana University Press, 1977), 5:33. Viganò actually used two numbers from Haydn's *Creation*—the depiction of chaos and the appearance of man in Uriel's aria, *In Native Worth and Honor Clad*— in his second presentation of the myth (1813).

[7]Ritorni, *Commentarii,* Libro primo, 47.

[8]A fairly recent work is actually titled *Il sogno del coreodramma: Salvatore Viganò, poeta muto,* written by Maria Nevilla Massaro and published by Mulino of Milan in 1984.

[9]Danced in the original production by a woman.

[10]The ballet is described in detail in Ritorni, *Commentarii,* 89-108 and in a scenario, *Prometeo, Ballo Mitologico,* published in Milan for the premiere.

A wealth of stage machinery[11] created aerial appearances and magical transformations. One continuous action melded the first three acts together. Gesture took the place of dialogue. Color and costume entranced the audience. Amid the scenes of grandeur, Viganò still managed to let dance technique become a way to a movement of the soul.[12] The ballet became the sensation of all of Italy. It merited a review in the *Allgemeine musikalische Zeitung*. It encouraged the prestigious house of Ricordi to began publishing piano scores for succeeding works.

Viganò gave up his dancing career; he devoted himself to choreography and worked methodically, without haste, for the realization of his ideas...He had a ballet rehearsed for months at a time. No matter if the first performance announced for spring could not take place until autumn. Often, in the midst of a rehearsal an idea came to him. He stopped everything and the artists waited entire hours for the maestro to indicate the manner of playing the scene...Before Viganò, the art of varied groupings was not known. In France as well as in Italy, the leader of the corps, the coryphée, executed expressive pantomime but the dancers and figurants were limited to performing all the same gestures. Suddenly the corps was divided into several groups each performing a different movement. With Viganò, each dancer preserved his individuality in the ensemble. One can imagine what work that had to be for the choreographer.[13]

Year by year, Viganò produced ballets on topics hitherto considered the province of drama or opera,[14] such works as *La Vestale* or *Otello*, ballets, complete art works, so extraordinary that he was commonly known as the Shakespeare of his day.[15]

This superb dancer/choreographer was far from the only artist finding correspondences within the arts. Paul Henry Lang has written a telling paragraph on the topic.

[11]According to the work of Mercedes Viale Ferrero, *La scenografia della Scala nell'età neoclassica* (Milan: Polifilo, 1983), 82, not many of the details of the scenography of *Prometeo* have been preserved—a pity because the concept demanded great splendor and ingenuity. Giacomo Preliasco designed the costumes, stage settings, and machines. Viale Ferrero includes two examples: Mercury in Flight (done by Preliasco) and the scene of the interior of a volcano (done by Giuseppe Galliari) as Plates xxx and xxxi.

[12]Henry Prunières, "Salvatore Viganò," *La Revue Musicale,* Numéro special: Le Ballet au XIXe siècle, December 1921:74-75.

[13]Prunières, "Viganò," 79.

[14]These are discussed by Elizabeth Terzian in "Salvatore Viganò: His Ballets at the Teatro La Scala (1811-1821)," (Master's thesis, University of California, Riverside, 1986). Terzian's article on Viganò in the *International Dictionary of Ballet* contains a fine appraisal of his achievements and a complete list of his ballets.

[15]Shakespeare with his ability to pierce to the innermost workings of the soul and body, his ability to explore the most complex emotions, became a symbol of what could be achieved in the new era.

Indeed, romanticism was engrossed with the idea of fusion of all arts; its poets painted, its painters made music, and its musicians painted and wrote dramas. The great historical canvases of the romantic painters needed literary elucidation, while correspondingly, mural painting blended with architecture. In the Pre-Raphaelites, music and poetry converged almost indivisibly, Daumier was a veritable painter-journalist; the novelists Stendhal, Balzac, Gautier, and Mérimée depicted their subjects with the exactitude of character painters; Goethe, E. T. A. Hoffmann, Stifter, and Mörike painted and composed. Kleist thought to find the secret of poetic form in counterpoint and pretended that his dramas were composed musically, the protagonists being more "voices" than figures. Swinburne's haunting, intoxicating and unrestrained lyrics are melodic in a musical sense, and the poet wanted them to be considered musical in nature; Whistler called his paintings "symphonies and nocturnes, harmonies in tone." On the other hand, the musicians turned to poetry and drama, and one of their ranks capped the whole century with his formidable, all-embracing Gesamtkunstwerk.[16]

Lang limited his paean to the nineteenth century but—taking the longer view of this essay—even in the half-century before 1800, before the full flowering of romanticism, many cultured artists had multiple interests similar to those that Lang noted. Goethe, talented in drawing, was already in the 1760s learning painting and would become known for contributions to color, perspective, acting, and directing. Rousseau followed a dual career of literature and music. Diderot, the progressive among the eighteenth-century group, published a musical treatise and became an authority on painting, theater, and acting. Fuseli is noted, among other things, for his painting of Shakepearean scenes. Houdon did his best work when inspired by the geniuses in the arts and sciences. Haydn had a small collection of engravings and was fascinated by literature of visual description.[17]

Just as Viganò did, Beethoven recognized that he could probe the subject of Prometheus beyond the realm of the initial "heroic-allegorical ballet" of 1801.[18] He expressed his dissatisfaction with that dance work in a letter to Hoffmeister, 22 April 1801, in which he wrote: "To say something of myself, I have just written a ballet in which the ballet-master did not do as well as he might have done."[19]

[16]Paul Henry Lang, *Music in Western Civilization* (New York: W. W. Norton, 1941), 736.

[17]Thomas Tolley, *Cannon's Roar* discusses the matter at length.

[18]Constantin Floros, *Beethovens Eroica und Prometheus-Musik*, Veröffentlichungen zur Musikforschung 3 (Wilhelmshaven: Heinrichshofen's Verlag, 1978), 30-34, contains a discussion of the various types of ballets. Alexander Wheelock Thayer, *Ludwig van Beethovens Leben*, ed. and enlarged Hugo Riemann, vols. 2-4 (Leipzig: Breitkopf & Härtel, 1910), 2:369-78 contains a table of the productions at the K. K. Hoftheater in Vienna, 1794-1805.

[19]Alexander Wheelock Thayer, *Thayer's Life of Beethoven*, rev. and ed. Elliot Forbes (Princeton, New Jersey: Princeton University, 1967), 273.

A critic for *Die Zeitung für die elegante Welt* recognized Beethoven's music as "für ein Ballet zu gelehrt", too learnèd for a ballet.[20] The recognition that emotions of substance must be as complex as those in the literary arts and that music must find means to express such deep feelings has already been shown in the Schubert and Mozart examples cited earlier.

Beethoven often gave written clues to the feeling tone aroused by his compositions. In the years before the Prometheus Ballet, he had titled one piano sonata *Pathétique* (Op. 13), called a movement *Marcia funebre sulla morte d'un Eroe* (Op. 26), designated another movement as *Largo e mesto* (Op. 10, No. 3), and marked two sonatas *quasi una fantasia* (Op. 27). He boldly incorporated dramatic slow introductions into the body of faster movements: (the Sixth String Quartet, Op. 18, with the "La Malinconia" introduction and in the Pathétique with the "Grave" introduction). To achieve such a close connection between technique and expression, he spent years pondering and polishing his musical materials— in the mind and in sketchbooks—before settling on the most faithful rendering of his idea which captured both significant musical substance *and* feeling tone.

He conceived of Prometheus as a great heroic figure, capable of helping mankind, worthy of profound expression.[21] Two of Beethoven's compositions from the ballet of 1801 proved to have lasting life. The introduction became his earliest well-known dramatic overture. The festive final dance contained a theme[22] that intrigued Beethoven so much that he continued to work on it[23] until his final capturing of its full essence in the Finale of the Eroica Symphony (composition in 1803, first public performance in 1805).

In indicating the expressive nature of a composition, a composer frequently relied upon words, correspondences, or even the sister art of literature. At times, in Beethoven's case, an adjective such as "Eroica" might suffice. At other times, a whole phrase such as "Heiliger Dankgesang eines Genesenen an die Gottheit, in der lydischen Tonart," A holy song of thanks from a convalescent to the godhead in the Lydian tonality (String Quartet, Op. 132) might be necessary. Finally, a complete fusion of literature and music might be required as in the vocal setting of Schiller's *An die Freude* in the Ninth Symphony.

This expressive quality in Beethoven's work was, and is, generally recognized—although with the caveat that it is difficult to describe the

---

[20]Review printed in Thayer, *Beethovens Leben,* 2: 237.

[21]Floros, *Beethovens Eroica,* 105-15 has shown quite conclusively that Beethoven associated the Titan with Napoleon, the original dedicatee of the Eroica.

[22]First known as a contradance for orchestra (WoO 14, No 7), it was evidently composed in 1801. Mollo published it in 1802 together with a transcription for piano.

[23]Breitkopf & Härtel published in 1803 a setting of this theme as a piano composition, Op. 35, *Variations on an Original Theme, Fifteen Variations and a Fugue* (composed 1802). The dual theme of bass ostinato and treble lyric melody suggested contrapuntal treatment and the fermata pause became an invitation to cadenzas and dramatic expansion.

indescribable in words.[24] Paul Bekker called it "the poetic idea."[25] Sir Donald Francis Tovey, noted for his technical analyses, recommended J. W. N. Sullivan's *Beethoven, His Spiritual Development* as a necessary supplement. Romain Rolland collected a group of "Beethoven's Thoughts," many bearing on this question.[26]

Beethoven's successors felt both the burden and the opportunity to achieve works of a similar high order, works endowed with something beyond consummate musical technique. In the season of 1839-40, three composers of outstanding talent used Beethovenian principles in new compositions. Their works, destined to become parts of the established repertory, received widespread notice and discussion. Berlioz in his *Roméo et Juliette* and Mendelssohn in his *Lobgesang* followed the Beethoven tradition of the choral symphony, a descriptive term welcomed by Berlioz whereas Mendelssohn searched for a another term and finally settled on "Symphony-Cantata." The third work, Schubert's *Die 7te Symphonie* [known today as the Great C Major Symphony], resurrected by Schumann, followed the motto-symphony tradition similar to that established in Beethoven's Fifth Symphony.

In the same season, Liszt, increasingly aware of the ferment in symphonic writing, decided on the path that he was to follow for the rest of his life. He sketched a Dante fragment and confided to his diary.

> If I feel within me the strength and life, I will attempt a symphonic composition based on Dante, then another on Faust—within three years—meanwhile I will make three sketches: the Triumph of Death (Orcagna), the Comedy of Death (Holbein), and a Fragment dantesque…The Pensieroso also bewitches me.[27]

Just after that season of 1839-1840, Wagner, newly alerted to dramatic trends in instrumental music, pondered his future too. He proposed that symphonic music would be more defined if combined with song and drama.

> Let us set the wild, unfettered elemental feelings, represented by the instruments, in contact with the clear and definite emotion of the human heart, as represented

---

[24]The difficulty was recognized by Beethoven in a letter to Wilhelm Gerhard, 15 July 1827, when he wrote, "The description of a picture belongs to painting. And in this respect the poet too, whose sphere in this case is not so restricted as mine, may consider himself to be more favoured than my Muse. On the other hand my sphere extends further into other regions and our empire cannot be so easily reached." (Emily Anderson, *Letters of Beethoven*, vol. 2 [London: Macmillan, 1961], 689). Beethoven never seems to have deviated from his own conviction and Neefe's instruction that the musician "depicts."

[25]Paul Bekker, *Beethoven*, trans. M. M. Bozman (London: J. M. Dent, 1925), Chap. 3.

[26]Romain Rolland, *Vie de Beethoven* (Paris: Hachette, 1945), 151-60.

[27]Liszt, "Journal des Zÿi," in d'Agoult *Mémoires*, 180, as translated by Sharon Winklhofer, "Liszt, Marie d'Agoult, and the 'Dante' Sonata," *19th Century Music* 1 (1977): 27. Liszt is one of the few composers who used visual themes in his music. The danger in that approach is that the compositions might easily turn into word-painting, a minor item in music's armory.

by the voice of man. The advent of this second element will calm and smooth the conflict of those primal feelings, will give their waves a definite, united course. Then the human heart opening to these complex emotions, enlarged and dilated by those infinite and pleasing presentiments, will welcome with rapture, with conviction, that kind of intimate revelation of a supernatural world.[28]

Before the year was out, he sketched *Der fliegende Holländer* in which operatic music was not only made semi-symphonic but even "visible" and intelligible in drama. In the following decade of the 1840s, the public found before it a series of works, some tending toward the "pure" symphonic and others toward the "dramatic." Some of the dramatic ones—Bochsa's *Die Gewalt der malenden Tonkunst* or Douay's *La Création, la Vie, et la Destruction, Symphonie poétique*—seemed to reach so far beyond the composer's powers as to suggest that the general movement toward the dramatic might be meretricious.[29] Others by Mendelssohn, Gade, and Schumann[30] proved of more value. Eventually in the 1850s, Liszt proposed a composition not as extended as a symphony but not as short as an overture, the symphonic poem—a term that combined the words for "sounding together" with the word for a "creation under divine fire." That genre and the operas of Wagner became major representatives of the new style.

All of the arts in the Late Promethean Period of 1850-1900 moved toward a highly charged state of emotion, toward topics drawn from powerful representations in the sister arts, and toward an encompassing approach that attempted to show the human condition in all its ranges. Courbet both shocked and intrigued his viewers with a view of a village funeral replete with a dog in the foreground and with a large group gathered at the open grave in the cemetary of Ornans. Hugo, himself a visual artist[31] as well as a literary man, tried to encompass the whole of human history in *La Légende des siècles*. Rodin wanted to achieve the ultimate goal of uniting his works into one grand unity, *La Porte de l'enfer*, a Dantesque view of the unity of life and death. Novelists such as George Eliot or Emile Zola wrote of whole families, their triumphs and disasters.

[28]Richard Wagner, "Une Visite à Beethoven, épisode de la vie d'un musicien allemand;" the quotation drawn from W. A. Ellis, *Richard Wagner's Prose Works*, 8 vols. (London: Routledge, Kegan Paul, 1894-99), 7:42. Wagner's original essay was printed in *La Revue et gazette musicale de Paris* during November and December of 1840. Note the similarity in title to Berlioz's *Symphonie fantastique, l'épisode de la vie d'un artiste* that however used the honored term of artist. This Wagner quotation, the previous one of Liszt, and the interpretation of them are drawn from my work in progress on the symphony from 1839 to 1850, that considers various attempts at the "dramatic" as it moved toward the symphonic poem.

[29]Scores for these works have disappeared but reviews and comparisons with known compositions do not suggest that we are in the presence of master works.

[30]Mendelssohn's *Symphonie in A Moll* [known today as the Scottish Symphony] and *Die erste Walpurgisnacht*, Gade's *Sinfonie in C Moll* [called the Great Northern Symphony]; and Schumann's *Symphonie in B Dur* and *Das Paradies und die Peri*.

[31]Pierre Georgel, "Le romantisme des années 1860," *Revue de l'Art* 20 (1973): 8-64. Pierre Georgel, *Drawings by Victor Hugo, Catalogue* (London: Victoria and Albert Museum, 1974).

Now, we have come full circle from Batteux's conviction that all of the arts derived from "a single principle," that of imitation. In actuality, the arts reached a state of notable unity through their personal expressive ideals, through their ever-increasing technical means, and through their devotion to "correspondences"—means not dreamed of by Batteux—but not far from his fundamental concept that the arts should be considered as an entity. Batteux expressed that unity and he also foretold it.

Artists now "lived" their own works over extended periods of time that were necessary for the gestation and birth of their large-scale conceptions. Wagner found his Isolde in Mathilde Wesendonck. Courbet knew well his native village of Ornans and sketched some of the characters in his funeral scene from life. Rodin let his models wander throughout the grounds of his *hôtel* and would constantly sketch them in clay.

The expressive ideal of the era, art works that evoked character, emotion and drama, had reached such an extreme intensity that a reaction was inevitable. A new cycle was to dawn at the turn from the nineteenth to the twentieth century with Debussy's "fresh air," the painter's moments *en plein air*, and especially with a concentration on the very materials of the art *per se* which led the new twentieth-century age into a delight in abstraction and away from the glories of the Promethean Age. For a time, promethean music—usually referred to as "Late Romantic," glorious compositions by Strauss, Mahler, or Rachmaninoff, musical tapestries with lush textures—continued to be written and performed.[32]

A new admiration for leanness of texture began to supplant the "by now swollen" promethean approach. The twentieth-century era turned more toward a use of artistic elements as abstract units. Those who had savored the promethean artistry looked back with nostalgia and regret. Even the musical language, the cultivation of melody expressed in uniform song-like phrases, seemed to have vanished together with its partner, lyric poetry. William Butler Yeats gently declared the "great song" faded and gone in a small poem, only a quatrain, "The Nineteenth Century and After."[33]

> Though the great song return no more
> There's keen delight in what we have,
> The rattle of pebbles on the shore
> Under the receding wave.

---

[32]The emotional world of promethean music is still very much alive today in the background music for films.

[33]W. B. Yeats, *The Poems*, ed. Richard J. Finneran, rev. ed. (New York: Scribner, 1997), 244. The title itself derives from the monthly review founded in 1877, a journal called *The Nineteenth Century*. When another century arrived, the journal's title was changed to *The Nineteenth Century and After*, a title used until 1951 when the editors belatedly renamed it *The Twentieth Century*.

9. Coda

Music took an honored place among the newly-recognized fine arts. It was essential to the frequently sought union of the arts. Musical techniques themselves changed significantly from their immediate baroque past. The older use of musical patterns and figures in contrapuntal/harmonic procedures gave way to expansive formal structures in melodic/harmonic procedures. Equally important, the baroque "expressive ideal," based on the doctrine of relatively stable affections and the presentation of a single affection at a time changed in the new era to a doctrine of character and to the presentation of mutating character often expressed in interactive dramatic ways. Music now reached out to vast new audiences of the industrial and democratic societies. The promethean expressive ideal lay behind the outpouring of remarkable operatic, vocal, chamber, keyboard, and symphonic works.

The new age, however, has till now lacked a generic title. It has generally been conceived as a duality[1] showing aspects of classic or romantic styles. In considering the era from 1750 to 1900—that "same historical period" and "one self-contained age"—Blume concluded:

> There is neither a "Classic" nor a "Romantic" style in music. Both aspects and both trends are continually merging into one. And as there are no discernible styles, there can neither be a clearly definable borderline between Classicism and Romanticism nor a distinct chronology of when the one or the other begins or ends.

So long as we keep the common generic terms, Classic and Romantic, as our *only* names[2] for the era, it will be impossible to move beyond Blume's flexible—but unnameable—view. Only in finding a new and inclusive term for the era can we name the age.

The Titan, Prometheus, with his concern for both technology and humanity can be an appropriate symbol of an age encompassing both the industrial and democratic revolutions. Music and the arts did not just passively

---

[1] All ages show a duality, the old and new mingle together. The new gradually asserts itself and the old declines in importance.
[2] I would reiterate that Classic and Romantic are important terms, hallowed by usage and much used by performers, artists, critics, and historians. They should not be jettisoned. My proposal includes them.

exist during the Promethean Era. They became shaped by the huge increase in population, by the expansion of technology, by the forces for public education, and by the values given to personal expression. Like all the forces of the age, they experienced synergy and the feeding upon themselves that accelerated the development of new outlooks and pushed their energy into all of Europe and ultimately into much of the world. The years of 1750 to 1900 saw a remarkable dissemination—of promethean proportions—of education, science, medicine, literature, and the fine arts, emerging into a human-centered freedom

"Promethean" serves well to characterize music in social and economic life of the time. It also serves well to welcome—with a freedom worthy of the Titan of ancient Greece—the many levels of music of the era, levels extending from the teaching piece, salon song, music hall number, or virtuoso pot boiler to gigantic operatic or symphonic works of profound workmanship and expression.

A single term such as the one proposed here—joined as it is to the mainstream of social, cultural, and political developments—would help to establish music as part of broader human history. The time has come to abandon the idea of music as an art *sui generis*. All too often the intricacies of musical construction have kept general historians from including music in their accounts of unfolding human endeavor. The converse is sometimes true. Occasionally the history of music has been presented as music literature with scant reference to the ebb and flow of society. The "new musicology," stressing cultural and social values in action and reaction with musical technique is already moving toward broader horizons. Researchers and several journals are recognizing the necessity for a "long century" concept in place of the exact limits of the nineteenth century. A further step would come if we could agree on a name for the era.

The era deserves a potent symbol, one that can encompass the vast technological and ideological changes of the age, one that can reflect the profound alteration in expressive ideals after the Baroque. Future detailed studies will reveal how comprehensive and useful *any* term can be for the 1750-1900 era, a span that encompassed the music of both Haydn and Brahms. Can the symbol for that musical age be Prometheus? Might the promethean message be, as Emerson said of language, "a part of the domain of knowledge—a new weapon in the magazine of power?"

Appendices

Appendix A

Two "popular" projects rivaled and supplemented the *Encylopédie*. The first, a multi-volume *Spectacle de la Nature* (1732-35, second edition 1749-51) is by the Abbé Noël-Antoine Pluche. His subtitle, "Conversations on the Details of Natural History Which Have Appeared Most Suitable to Make Young People Curious and to Form Their Minds," suggests the wide audience that he cultivated. The work is illustrated by inserted foldouts showing such things as housing and even furniture. The range of material in the second edition extends to the "arts" which he discusses under the rubrics of "arts which instruct mankind" and the "instructive professions." The "Conversations" went out to an eager audience. See D. Trinkle, "Noël-Antoine Pluche's *Le Spectacle de la nature*: an Encyclopaedic Best Seller," *Studies on Voltaire and the Eighteenth Century* No. 358 (1997): 93-134 and Benoit de Baere, *Trois Introductions à l'Abbé Pluche. sa vie, son monde, ses livres* (Geneva: Droz, 2001). A "popular" work such as this is often omitted from the usual readings in aesthetics; however, from the promethean viewpoint and also from that of modern scholarship, the transmission of information to large numbers of people is a significant part of the changes taking place in this age.

The second encyclopedic work is the *Histoire naturelle* (44 volumes, 1749-1804) by the Comte de Buffon. A highly variable work, one portion adumbrated the theories of evolution whereas others were not completely to be trusted. Buffon, in his *Discourse on Style* at his elevation to the Académie Française, embraced the concept of human feeling (*sentiment*) in his elegant statement that "style is the man himself."

Beyond these two encyclopedic works, there is yet a third pertinent item that should be mentioned. It consists of a series of path-breaking studies of Alexander von Humboldt (1769-1859), the scientist/humanist whose expeditions in Spain, South America, Central America, and Russia gave detailed geographical and ethnic accounts that almost single-handedly created the field of geography and allied sciences. Daniel Johnson in "From a lost world," *Times Literary Supplement*, 22 July 2005:3, states "Not only did he invent or reinvent several new branches of earth and life sciences (including human and plant geography, climatology and vulcanology, hydrology, and geomagnetism) and greatly augment most others, he also transformed the historiography and philosophy of science.

We owe to him such familiar scientific notions as the isothermal lines on weather maps, seismic waves, magnetic storms, reverse polarity, the Jurassic era." In addition, Humboldt embraced the dawning sense of humanity—particularly as found in the work of Goethe and Schiller. He promoted equality among races, dispelled many prejudices, fostered democracy, and supported his brother Wilhelm's work in education. In the latter part of his life, he completed an encyclopedic work, *Kosmos, Entwurf einer physischen Weltbeschreibung* that not only described in detail the physical world but its interaction with the human world. Humboldt represents the fusion of material knowledge and the sense of humanity that is the basis of the present essay.

Appendix B

The influence of Burke on Diderot is discussed in Gita May, "Diderot and Burke: A Study in Aesthetic Affinity," *Publications of the Modern Language Association* (December 1960), 527-39. Schiller wrote two essays on the sublime (1763, 1801) and Kant wrote an extended essay, *Beobachtungen über das Gefühl des Schönen und Erhabenen* (1763). The awe-inspiring strength of the sublime in nature—and the sublime in music—is conveyed by Schiller's poem, *Die Macht des Gesanges*, The Power of Song, published with a musical setting in *Der Musen-Almanach* for 1796:

Ein Regenstrom aus Felsenrissen	A stream of rain from rocky cliffs,
Er kommt mit Donners Ungestüm	Comes with monstrous thunder,
Bergtrümmer folgen seinen Güssen,	Mountain fragments follow its torrents
Und Eichen stürzen unter ihm,	And oaks crash down under it,
Erstaunt mit wollustrollen Graussen	Astonished with lustful dread
Hört ihn der Wanderer und lauscht,	The wanderer hears it and listens,
Er hört die Flut vom Felsen brausen,	He hears the flood roar from the rocks
Doch weiss er nicht, woher sie rauscht;	But knows not from where it rushes;
So strömen des Gesanges Wellen	Just so, song's waves stream
Hervor aus nie entdeckten Quellen.	Forth from yet undiscovered sources.

Appendix C

The term *expression* was used in the Baroque Age in France. We have seen it in the title of the Le Brun *Conference*; however, it was still associated with the stability of the representations of the passions. In the Promethean Age it became associated with the new ideal of representation of *sentiment* (feelings), Expression was defined in the *Encylopédie* in this manner: "Music is an imitation and is, and can be, only the expressive imitation of the feeling (*sentiment*) that is depicted." The term *expression* in English according to the *Oxford Dictionary* as a "fact or way of expressing character, sentiment, action, etc." came into use first in regard to visual art by Jonathan Richardson the Elder in *An Essay on the Theory of Painting* in 1715. In regard to music it was first used as a judgment on the singing of birds as "expression is wanting, without which music is so languid and inanimate" by Daines Barrington in *Philosophical Transactions,* LXIII, 288 in "Experiments and Observations on the Singing of Birds," in 1773. The Grimm *Deutsches Wörterbuch* defines *Ausdruck* as a word that first sprung up in the eighteenth century with the "sense of the French and English word *expression.*"

Appendix D

Coupled with this delight in song was a great wave of lyric poetry. Sometimes the two went their independent ways but much of the time they found themselves progressing in tandem. Many poets had a vivid interest in lyric poetry's connection with song. Herder found a renewal of German art in folk song and folk poetry in his publications from 1773 on. Through his close connections with Goethe, he was able to influence that master toward folk-like simplicity for lyric poems. It became, for a period of time, rather fashionable for poets to write new texts to songs already known. Frederick W. Sternfeld has published a study detailing the writing of new texts to folk music: *Goethe and Music, A List of Parodies and Goethe's Relationship to Music* (New York: New York Public Library, 1954).

Goethe and Wieland edited an almanac under the title *Taschenbuch auf das Jahr 1804* in two versions, one of the poetry alone and the other in a version of songs with guitar accompaniment. A small discussion of this musical *Taschenbuch* and an illustration of its cover page occurs in Maria Gräfin Lanckoronska and Dr. Arthur Rümann's *Geschichte der Deutschen Taschenbücher und Almanache aus der klassisch-romantischen Zeit* (Munich: Ernst Heimeran, 1954). This work chronicles many types of pocket books and almanacs: those for musical people, for women, for children, etc.

Appendix E

A considerable gulf existed between the simple keyboard style and the symphonic style. The more complex style required a composer trained and skilled in all aspects of harmony, modulation, counterpoint and orchestration; whereas, the simple style required a composer with a sense of melody and rudimentary harmony—the latter derived as much from observation of common use as from theoretical study. Emanuel Bach's terms, *Kenner* and *Liebhaber*, connoisseur and amateur, two words in opposition to each other —although admitting many gradations within each category—come closest to describing the situation.

The noun *connoisseur*—used in the sense of a critical judge of the fine arts or a judge in matters of taste—dates from just before this time period. The noun, *amateur*, in the sense of one who loves something or has a taste for it—sometimes with the connotation of being attracted to something as a pastime—is contemporary with this era. The *New Oxford Dictionary* dates "amateur" as 1784, a usage from the French, and dates "connoisseur" as 1714.

The Robert *Dictionnaire historique de la langue française* dates "amateur" as one "qui aime un art sans en faire sa profession" as 1782 and "connaisseur" from a usage by Molière in 1670. The *Dictionnaire universel* (known as the *Dictionnaire de Trévoux*) in its 1752 edition introduced many new words and included a famous statement that while one could be an amateur without being a connoisseur, it was impossible to be a connoisseur without being an amateur—that is, a "lover" of art. The *Grand Larousse de la langue française* places "amateur" a little earlier at the end of the seventeenth century. The Grimm *Deutsches Wörterbuch* cites uses of "Liebhaber" as "der eine Person lieb hat, Freund, Verehrer" as do the other language dictionaries and cites Winckelmann speaking "von diesem Liebhaber und Kenner der Künste" and quotes, in addition, other eighteenth-century writers such as Arnim and Goethe.

Index

12 *n* 1 =footnote page followed by footnote number
italic number = title or illustration

INDEX

Kosmos (Humboldt), 84

LaBorde, Benjamin *Choix de Chansons, 46,* 47

Lang, Paul Henry fusion of the arts, 76

Late Promethean Period, 49-50

Late Romantic compositions, 80

LeBrun, Charles, *2*

libraries, 8

Lieder im Volkston, 55

Lied through-composed, 53

Liszt, Franz, 11, 28-29, 78

literacy, 7, 35, 40

lullaby, 56

Martin, Richard and protection of animals, 7

Marx, Karl use of Prometheus as symbol, 29-30

melody simple and natural, 51-52, of three notes, 56, after the Promethean Era, 80

Middle Promethean Period, 49

Moreau le jeune (illustrator), 47

Mozart, Leopold violin method, 63

Mozart, Wolfgang Amadeus piano concerto K482, 68-71

Musenalmanach, Wienerischer, 62

music dealers, 42 *n* 22

nature poetry in a song, 55

Neefe, Christian Gottlob on the great artist and the bungler, 66

Oberlin, Friedrich as reformer, 7

ode, 52

Orphéon, 17, 17 *n* 22, *34*

Palisca, Claude expressive ideal of the Baroque, 3

Parnasse François, 28

Père Lachaise (cemetery), 28

periodical overture, *72*

periodicals, 40

periodicity, 64-65

Pestalozzi, Johann Heinrich, 49

Philosophical Enquiry into the Origins of our Ideas of the Sublime and the Beautiful (Burke), 27 *n* 21

piano, 15-18, and harpsichord, 16

Pluche, Abbé Noël-Antoine and *Spectacle de la nature,* 83

poetry and music, 27, 87

Poet's Corner, 28

population increase, 33-34

Power of Music and Dance ballet (Viganò-Beethoven), 74

Prometeo (Viganò), 74

Promethean Era literature, 23 *n* 7, problems, excesses, and contradictions, 30-31, new power, 71

Prometheus (Titan, the Forethinker), 11, *12, 22, 54,* 81, as symbol, 29-31, *Der entfesselte Prometheus* (Herder), 31, 31 *n, 35,* in song, 53, as subject of ballets, 74-75, *Die Geschöpfe des Prometheus* (Viganò-Beethoven), 74

Prometheus (Goethe), 30

Prometheus Unbound (Shelley), 29

prints, 40, *41*

Prunières, Henry on ballet 75

publishing, 18-19, 22, 42 *n* 22, serial publishing, 22, 40, 42 *n* 22, 71, *72,* La Chevardière, 38, *38*

Quantz, Johann Joachim and his *Versuch,* 63-64

Rainbow, Bernarr classic texts in music education, 35 *n* 5

Ramler, Carl Wilhelm and German song, 52-53

reformers, social, 29-30

RISM, 19

romantic (style term), 5-6, 9, 80-81

Rosen, Charles *The Classical Style,* 48-49

Rousseau, Jean-Jacques collection of prints, 40, melody, 52, melody of three notes, 56, lower opinion of instrumental music, 64 *n* 7